10-23-72

JOHN LOTHROP MOTLEY.

JOHN LOTHROP MOTLEY.

A MEMOIR.

BY

OLIVER WENDELL HOLMES.

BOOKS FOR LIBRARIES PRESS
FREEPORT, NEW YORK

First Published 1878
Reprinted 1972

INTERNATIONAL STANDARD BOOK NUMBER:
0-8369-6775-5

LIBRARY OF CONGRESS CATALOG CARD NUMBER:
71-38358

PRINTED IN THE UNITED STATES OF AMERICA
BY
NEW WORLD BOOK MANUFACTURING CO., INC.
HALLANDALE, FLORIDA 33009

INTRODUCTORY NOTE.

THE Memoir here given to the public is based on a biographical sketch prepared by the writer at the request of the Massachusetts Historical Society for its Proceedings. The questions involving controversies into which the Society could not feel called to enter are treated at considerable length in the following pages. Many details are also given which would have carried the paper written for the Society beyond the customary limits of such tributes to the memory of its deceased members. It is still but an outline which may serve a present need and perhaps be of some assistance to a future biographer.

CONTENTS.

APPENDIX.

JOHN LOTHROP MOTLEY.

I.

Birth and Early Years. (1814-1827.)

SECTION I.

Ancestry.

JOHN MOTLEY, the great-grandfather of the subject of this Memoir, came in the earlier part of the last century from Belfast in Ireland to Falmouth, now Portland, in the District, now the State of Maine. He was twice married, and had ten children, four of the first marriage and six of the last. Thomas, the youngest son by his first wife, married Emma, a daughter of John Wait, the first Sheriff of Cumberland County under the government of the United States. Two of their seven sons, Thomas and Edward, removed from Portland to Boston in 1802 and established themselves as partners in commercial business, continuing united and prosperous for nearly half a century before the firm was dissolved.

The earlier records of New England have preserved the memory of an incident which deserves

Section I.

Ancestry.

mention as showing how the historian's life was saved by a quick-witted handmaid, more than a hundred years before he was born. On the 29th of August, 1708, the French and Indians from Canada made an attack upon the town of Haverhill, in Massachusetts. Thirty or forty persons were slaughtered, and many others were carried captive into Canada.

The minister of the town, Rev. Benjamin Rolfe, was killed by a bullet through the door of his house. Two of his daughters, Mary, aged thirteen, and Elizabeth, aged nine, were sleeping in a room with the maid-servant, Hagar. When Hagar heard the whoop of the savages she seized the children, ran with them into the cellar, and, after concealing them under two large washtubs, hid herself. The Indians ransacked the cellar, but missed the prey. Elizabeth, the younger of the two girls, grew up and married the Rev. Samuel Checkley, first minister of the "New South" Church, Boston. Her son, Rev. Samuel Checkley, Junior, was minister of the Second Church, and his successor, Rev. John Lothrop, or Lathrop, as it was more commonly spelled, married his daughter. Dr. Lothrop was great-grandson of Rev. John Lothrop, of Scituate, who had been imprisoned in England for nonconformity. The Checkleys were from Preston Capes, in Northamptonshire. The name is probably identical with that of the Chicheles or Chichleys, a well-known Northamptonshire family.

Thomas Motley married Anna, daughter of the Rev. John Lothrop, granddaughter of the Rev. Samuel Checkley, Junior, the two ministers mentioned above, both honored in their day and generation. Eight children were born of this marriage, of whom four are still living.

Birth.

JOHN LOTHROP MOTLEY, the second of these children, was born in Dorchester, now a part of Boston, Massachusetts, on the 15th of April, 1814. A member of his family gives a most pleasing and interesting picture, from his own recollections and from what his mother told him, of the childhood which was to develop into such rich maturity. The boy was rather delicate in organization, and not much given to outdoor amusements, except skating and swimming, of which last exercise he was very fond in his young days, and in which he excelled. He was a great reader, never idle, but always had a book in his hand, — a volume of poetry or one of the novels of Scott or Cooper. His fondness for plays and declamation is illustrated by the story told by a younger brother, who remembers being wrapped up in a shawl and kept quiet by sweetmeats, while he figured as the dead Cæsar, and his brother, the future historian, delivered the speech of

Childhood.

Antony over his prostrate body. He was of a most sensitive nature, easily excited, but not tenacious of any irritated feelings, with a quick sense of honor, and the most entirely truthful child, his mother used to say, that she had ever seen. Such are some of the recollections of those who knew him in his earliest years and in the most intimate relations.

Early character.

His father's family was at this time living in the house No. 7 Walnut Street, looking down Chestnut Street over the water to the western hills. Near by, at the corner of Beacon Street, was the residence of the family of the first Mayor of Boston, and at a little distance from the opposite corner was the house of one of the fathers of New England manufacturing enterprise, a man of superior intellect, who built up a great name and fortune in our city. The children from these three homes naturally became playmates. Mr. Motley's house was a very hospitable one, and Lothrop and two of his young companions were allowed to carry out their schemes of amusement in the garden and the garret. If one with a prescient glance could have looked into that garret on some Saturday afternoon while our century was not far advanced in its second score of years, he might have found three boys in cloaks and doublets and plumed hats, heroes and bandits, enacting more or less impromptu melodramas. In

Playmates.

Playmates.

one of the boys he would have seen the embryo dramatist of a nation's life history, John Lothrop Motley; in the second, a famous talker and wit who has spilled more good things on the wasteful air in conversation than would carry a "diner-out" through half a dozen London seasons, and waked up somewhat after the usual flowering-time of authorship to find himself a very agreeable and cordially welcomed writer, — Thomas Gold Appleton. In the third he would have recognized a champion of liberty known wherever that word is spoken, an orator whom to hear is to revive all the traditions of the grace, the address, the commanding sway of the silver-tongued eloquence of the most renowned speakers, — Wendell Phillips.

Both of young Motley's playmates have furnished me with recollections of him and of those around him at this period of his life, and I cannot do better than borrow freely from their communications.

His father.

His father was a man of decided character, social, vivacious, witty, a lover of books, and himself not unknown as a writer, being the author of one or more of the well-remembered "Jack Downing" letters. He was fond of having the boys read to him from such authors as Channing and Irving, and criticised their way of reading with discriminating judgment and taste. Mrs. Motley was a

SECTION I. 1814-1827.

His mother.

woman who could not be looked upon without admiration. I remember well the sweet dignity of her aspect, her "regal beauty," as Mr. Phillips truly styles it, and the charm of her serene and noble presence, which made her the type of a perfect motherhood. Her character corresponded to the promise of her gracious aspect. She was one of the fondest of mothers, but not thoughtlessly indulgent to the boy from whom she hoped and expected more than she thought it wise to let him know. The story used to be current that in their younger days this father and mother were the handsomest pair the town of Boston could show. This son of theirs was "rather tall," says Mr. Phillips, "lithe, very graceful in movement and gesture, and there was something marked and admirable in the set of his head on his shoulders," — a peculiar elegance which was most noticeable in those later days when I knew him. Lady Byron long afterwards spoke of him as more like her husband in appearance than any other person she had met; but Mr. Phillips, who remembers the first bloom of his boyhood and youth, thinks he was handsomer than any portrait of Byron represents the poet. "He could not have been eleven years old," says the same correspondent, "when he began writing a novel. It opened, I remember, not with one solitary horseman, but

His early beauty.

Begins a novel.

Section I. 1814-1827.

with two, riding up to an inn in the valley of the Housatonic. Neither of us had ever seen the Housatonic, but it sounded grand and romantic. Two chapters were finished."

At school.

There is not much remembered of the single summer he passed at Mr. Green's school at Jamaica Plain. From that school he went to Round Hill, Northampton, then under the care of Mr. Cogswell and Mr. Bancroft. The historian of the United States could hardly have dreamed that the handsome boy of ten years old was to take his place at the side of his teacher in the first rank of writers in his own department. Motley came to Round Hill, as one of his schoolmates tells me, with a great reputation, especially as a declaimer. He had a remarkable facility for acquiring languages, excelled as a reader and as a writer, and was the object of general admiration for his many gifts. There is some reason to think that the flattery he received was for a time a hindrance to his progress and the development of his character. He obtained praise too easily, and learned to trust too much to his genius. He had everything to spoil him, — beauty, precocious intelligence, and a personal charm which might have made him a universal favorite. Yet he does not seem to have been generally popular at this period of his life. He was wilful, impetuous,

Flattered for his gifts.

Section I. 1814-1827.

sometimes supercilious, always fastidious. He would study as he liked, and not by rule. His school and college mates believed in his great possibilities through all his forming period, but it may be doubted if those who counted most confidently on his future could have supposed that he would develop the heroic power of concentration, the long-breathed tenacity of purpose, which in after years gave effect to his brilliant mental endowments. "I did wonder," says Mr. Wendell Phillips, "at the diligence and painstaking, the drudgery shown in his historical works. In early life he had no industry, not needing it. All he cared for in a book he caught quickly, — the spirit of it, and all his mind needed or would use. This quickness of apprehension was marvellous." I do not find from the recollections of his schoolmates at Northampton that he was reproached for any grave offences, though he may have wandered beyond the prescribed boundaries now and then, and studied according to his inclinations rather than by rule. While at that school he made one acquisition much less common then than now, — a knowledge of the German language and some degree of acquaintance with its literature, under the guidance of one of the few thorough German scholars this country then possessed, Mr. George Bancroft.

Learned easily.

Studied what he chose.

II.

College Life. (*1827 - 1831.*)

SECTION II.
1827 - 1831.

College life.

SUCH then was the boy who at the immature, we might almost say the tender, age of thirteen entered Harvard College. Though two years after me in college standing, I remember the boyish reputation which he brought with him, especially that of a wonderful linguist, and the impression which his striking personal beauty produced upon us as he took his seat in the college chapel. But it was not until long after this period that I became intimately acquainted with him, and I must again have recourse to the classmates and friends who have favored me with their reminiscences of this period of his life. Mr. Phillips says: "During our first year in college, though the youngest in the class, he stood third, I think, or second in college rank, and ours was an especially able class. Yet to maintain this rank he neither cared nor needed to make any effort. Too young to feel any responsibilities, and not yet awake to any ambition, he became so negligent that he was 'rusticated' [that is, sent away from college for a time]. He came back sobered,

College rank.

SECTION II. 1827 - 1831.

and worked rather more, but with no effort for college rank thenceforward."

College life.

I must finish the portrait of the collegian with all its lights and shadows by the help of the same friends from whom I have borrowed the preceding outlines. He did not care to make acquaintances, was haughty in manner and cynical in mood, at least as he appeared to those in whom he felt no special interest. It is no wonder, therefore, that he was not a popular favorite, although recognized as having very brilliant qualities. During all this period his mind was doubtless fermenting with projects which kept him in a fevered and irritable condition. "He had a small writing-table," Mr. Phillips says, "with a shallow drawer; I have often seen it half full of sketches, unfinished poems, soliloquies, a scene or two of a play, prose portraits of some pet character, etc. These he would read to me, though he never volunteered to do so, and every now and then he burnt the whole and began to fill the drawer again."

His manner.

His literary attempts.

My friend, Mr. John Osborne Sargent, who was a year before him in college, says, in a very interesting letter with which he has favored me: "My first acquaintance with him [Motley] was at Cambridge, when he came from Mr. Cogswell's school at Round Hill. He then had a good deal of the shyness that was just pronounced enough to make him interesting, and which did not entirely wear off till he left college. . . . . I soon became acquainted with him, and we used to take long walks together, sometimes taxing each other's memory for poems or passages from poems that had struck our fancy. Shelley was then a great favorite of his, and I remember that Praed's verses then appearing in the New Monthly he thought very clever and brilliant, and was fond of repeating them. You have forgotten, or perhaps never knew, that Motley's first appearance in print was in the 'Collegian.' He brought me one day, in a very modest mood, a translation from Goethe, which I was most happy to oblige him by inserting. It was very prettily done, and will now be a curiosity. . . . . How it happened that Motley wrote only one piece I do not remember. I had the pleasure about that time of initiating him as a member of the Knights of the Square Table, — always my favorite college club, for the reason, perhaps, that I was a sometime Grand Master. He was always a genial and jovial companion at our supper-parties at Fresh Pond and Gallagher's."

College life.

His poetical favorites.

His first appearance in print.

We who live in the days of photographs know how many faces belong to every individual. We know too under what different aspects the same character appears to those who study it from different points of view and with different preposses-

SECTION II. 1827-1831.

College life.

sions. I do not hesitate, therefore, to place side by side the impressions of two of his classmates as to one of his personal traits as they observed him at this period of his youth.

Not particular as to dress.

"He was a manly boy, with no love for or leaning to girls' company; no care for dress; not a trace of personal vanity. . . . . He was, or at least seemed, wholly unconscious of his rare beauty and of the fascination of his manner; not a trace of pretence, the simplest and most natural creature in the world."

Look on that picture and on this:

A different account.

"He seemed to have a passion for dress. But as in everything else, so in this, his fancy was a fitful one. At one time he would excite our admiration by the splendor of his outfit, and perhaps the next week he would seem to take equal pleasure in his slovenly or careless appearance."

The accounts reconciled.

It is not very difficult to reconcile these two portraitures. I recollect it was said by a witty lady of a handsome clergyman well remembered among us, that he had *dressy eyes.* Motley so well became everything he wore, that if he had sprung from his bed and slipped his clothes on at an alarm of fire, his costume would have looked like a prince's undress. His natural presentment, like that of Count D'Orsay, was of the kind which suggests the intentional effects of an elaborate toilet, no matter how little thought or care may have been given to make it effective. I think the "passion for dress" was really only a seeming, and that he often excited admiration when he had not taken half the pains to adorn himself that many a youth less favored by nature has wasted upon his unblest exterior only to be laughed at.

College life.

I gather some other interesting facts from a letter which I have received from his early playmate and school and college classmate, Mr. T. G. Appleton.

"In his Sophomore year he kept abreast of the prescribed studies, but his heart was out of bounds, as it often had been at Round Hill when chasing squirrels or rabbits through forbidden forests. Already his historical interest was shaping his life. A tutor coming — by chance, let us hope — to his room, remonstrated with him upon the heaps of novels upon his table.

Novel-reading.

"'Yes,' said Motley, 'I am reading historically, and have come to the novels of the nineteenth century. Taken in the lump, they are very hard reading.'"

All Old Cambridge people know the Brattle House, with its gambrel roof, its tall trees, its perennial spring, its legendary fame of good fare and hospitable board in the days of the kindly old *bon vivant*, Major Brattle. In this house the two young students, Appleton and Motley, lived during a part of their college course.

Room at the "Brattle House."

SECTION II. 1827-1831.

College life.

"Motley's room was on the ground floor, the room to the left of the entrance. He led a very pleasant life there, tempering his college duties with the literature he loved, and receiving his friends amidst elegant surroundings, which added to the charm of his society. Occasionally we amused ourselves by writing for the magazines and papers of the day. Mr. Willis had just started a slim monthly, written chiefly by himself, but with the true magazine flavor. We wrote for that, and sometimes verses in the corner of a paper called the Anti-Masonic Mirror, and in which corner was a woodcut of Apollo, and inviting to destruction ambitious youths by the legend underneath,

Writes for magazines and papers.

'Much yet remains unsung.'

These pieces were usually dictated to each other, the poet recumbent upon the bed and a classmate ready to carry off the manuscript for the paper of the following day. Blackwood's was then in its glory, its pages redolent of 'mountain dew' in every sense; the humor of the Shepherd, the elegantly brutal onslaughts upon Whigs and Cockney poets by Christopher North, intoxicated us youths.

"It was young writing, and made for the young. The opinions were charmingly wrong, and its enthusiasm was half Glenlivet. But this delighted the boys. There were no reprints then, and to pass the paper-cutter up the fresh inviting pages was like swinging over the heather arm in arm with Christopher himself. It is a little singular that though we had a college magazine of our own, Motley rarely if ever wrote for it. I remember a translation from Goethe, 'The Ghost-Seer,' which he may have written for it, and a poem upon the White Mountains. Motley spoke at one of the college exhibitions an essay on Goethe so excellent that Mr. Joseph Cogswell sent it to Madam Goethe, who, after reading it, said, 'I wish to see the first book that young man will write.'"

College life.

Writes poems.

Writes an essay on Goethe.

Although Motley did not aim at or attain a high college rank, the rules of the Phi Beta Kappa Society, which confine the number of members to the first sixteen of each class, were stretched so as to include him,—a tribute to his recognized ability, and an evidence that a distinguished future was anticipated for him.

III.

Study and Travel in Europe. (*1832-1833.*)

SECTION III. 1832-1833.

Studies in Germany.

OF the two years divided between the Universities of Berlin and Göttingen I have little to record. That he studied hard I cannot doubt; that he found himself in pleasant social relations with some of his fellow-students seems probable from the portraits he has drawn in his first story, "Morton's Hope," and is rendered certain so far as one of his companions is concerned. Among the records of the past to which he referred during his last visit to this country was a letter which he took from a collection of papers and handed me to read one day when I was visiting him. The letter was written in a very lively and exceedingly familiar vein. It implied such intimacy, and called up in such a lively way the gay times Motley and himself had had together in their youthful days, that I was puzzled to guess who could have addressed him from Germany in that easy and offhand fashion. I knew most of his old friends who would be likely to call him by his baptismal name in its

A letter from an early friend.

most colloquial form, and exhausted my stock of guesses unsuccessfully before looking at the signature. I confess that I was surprised, after laughing at the hearty and almost boyish tone of the letter, to read at the bottom of the page the signature of Bismarck. I will not say that I suspect Motley of having drawn the portrait of his friend in one of the characters of "Morton's Hope," but it is not hard to point out traits in one of them which we can believe may have belonged to the great Chancellor at an earlier period of life than that at which the world contemplates his overshadowing proportions.

Bismarck.

Hoping to learn something of Motley during the two years while we had lost sight of him, I addressed a letter to His Highness Prince Bismarck, to which I received the following reply:—

FOREIGN OFFICE, BERLIN, March 11, 1878.

Note from his secretary

SIR,—I am directed by Prince Bismarck to acknowledge the receipt of your letter of the 1st of January, relating to the biography of the late Mr. Motley. His Highness deeply regrets that the state of his health and pressure of business do not allow him to contribute personally, and as largely as he would be delighted to do, to your depicting of a friend whose memory will be ever dear to him. Since I had the pleasure of making the acquaint-

SECTION III.
1832–1833.

ance of Mr. Motley at Varzin, I have been intrusted with communicating to you a few details I have gathered from the mouth of the Prince. I enclose them as they are jotted down, without any attempt of digestion.

I have the honor to be
Your obedient servant,
LOTHAIR BUCHER.

"Prince Bismarck said: —

Prince Bismarck's recollections of Motley.

"'I met Motley at Göttingen in 1832, I am not sure if at the beginning of Easter Term or Michaelmas Term. He kept company with German students, though more addicted to study than we members of the fighting clubs (: corps :). Although not having mastered yet the German language, he exercised a marked attraction by a conversation sparkling with wit, humor, and originality. In autumn of 1833, having both of us migrated from Göttingen to Berlin for the prosecution of our studies, we became fellow-lodgers in the house No. 161 Friedrich Strasse. There we lived in the closest intimacy, sharing meals and outdoor exercise. Motley by that time had arrived at talking German fluently; he occupied himself not only in translating Goethe's poem "Faust," but tried his hand even in composing German verses. Enthusiastic admirer of Shakespeare, Byron, Goethe, he used to

Prince Bismarck's recollections

spice his conversation abundantly with quotations from these his favorite authors. A pertinacious arguer, so much so that sometimes he watched my awakening in order to continue a discussion on some topic of science, poetry, or practical life, cut short by the chime of the small hours, he never lost his mild and amiable temper. Our faithful companion was Count Alexander *Keyserling*, a native of Courland, who has since achieved distinction as a botanist.

"'Motley having entered the diplomatic service of his country, we had frequently the opportunity of renewing our friendly intercourse; at Frankfurt he used to stay with me, the welcome guest of my wife; we also met at Vienna, and, later, here. The last time I saw him was in 1872 at Varzin, at the celebration of my "silver wedding," namely, the twenty-fifth anniversary.

"'The most striking feature of his handsome and delicate appearance was uncommonly large and beautiful eyes. He never entered a drawing-room without exciting the curiosity and sympathy of the ladies.'"

The three companions.

It is but a glimpse of their young life which the great statesman gives us, but a bright and pleasing one. Here were three students, one of whom was to range in the flowery fields of the loveliest of the sciences, another to make the dead past live over again in his burning pages, and a third to extend an empire, as the botanist spread out a plant and the historian laid open a manuscript.

IV.

Return to America. — Study of Law. — Marriage. — His first Novel, "Morton's Hope." (1834 - 1839.)

SECTION IV. 1834 - 1839.

OF the years passed in the study of Law after his return from Germany I have very little recollection, and nothing of importance to record. He never became seriously engaged in the practice of the profession he had chosen. I had known him pleasantly rather than intimately, and our different callings tended to separate us. I met him, however, not very rarely, at one house where we were both received with the greatest cordiality, and where the attractions brought together many both young and old to enjoy the society of its charming and brilliant inmates. This was at No. 14 Temple Place, where Mr. Park Benjamin was then living with his two sisters, both in the bloom of young womanhood. Here Motley found the wife to whom his life owed so much of its success and its happiness. Those who remember Mary Benjamin find it hard to speak of her in the common terms of praise which they award to the good and the lovely. She was not only handsome and

My acquaintance with him.

The house where he was often to be met.

amiable and agreeable, but there was a cordial frankness, an open-hearted sincerity about her which made her seem like a sister to those who could help becoming her lovers. She stands quite apart in the memory of the friends who knew her best, even from the circle of young persons whose recollections they most cherish. Yet hardly could one of them have foreseen all that she was to be to him whose life she was to share. They were married on the 2d of March, 1837. His intimate friend, Mr. Joseph Lewis Stackpole, was married at about the same time to her sister, thus joining still more closely in friendship the two young men who were already like brothers in their mutual affection.

His marriage.

His first novel.

Two years after his marriage, in 1839, appeared his first work, a novel in two volumes, called "Morton's Hope." He had little reason to be gratified with its reception. The general verdict was not favorable to it, and the leading critical journal of America, not usually harsh or cynical in its treatment of native authorship, did not even give it a place among its "Critical Notices," but dropped a small-print extinguisher upon it in one of the pages of its "List of New Publications." Nothing could be more utterly disheartening than the unqualified condemnation passed upon the story. At the same time the critic says that "no one can read 'Morton's Hope' without perceiving it to have been written by a person of uncommon resources of mind and scholarship."

"Morton's Hope."

It must be confessed that, as a story, "Morton's Hope" cannot endure a searching or even a moderately careful criticism. It is wanting in cohesion, in character, even in a proper regard to circumstances of time and place; it is a map of dissected incidents which has been flung out of its box and has arranged itself without the least regard to chronology or geography. It is not difficult to trace in it many of the influences which had helped in forming or deforming the mind of the young man of twenty-five, not yet come into possession of his full inheritance of the slowly ripening qualities which were yet to assert their robust independence. How could he help admiring Byron and falling into more or less unconscious imitation of his moods if not of his special affectations? Passion showing itself off against a dark foil of cynicism; sentiment, ashamed of its own self-betrayal, and sneering at itself from time to time for fear of the laugh of the world at its sincerity,—how many young men were spoiled and how many more injured by becoming bad copies of a bad ideal! The blood of Don Juan ran in the veins of Vivian Grey and of Pelham. But if we read the fantastic dreams of Disraeli, the intellectual dandyisms of Bulwer,

SECTION IV. 1839.

"Morton's Hope."

remembering the after careers of which these were the preludes, we can understand how there might well be something in those earlier efforts which would betray itself in the way of thought and in the style of the young men who read them during the plastic period of their minds and characters. Allow for all these influences, allow for whatever impressions his German residence and his familiarity with German literature had produced; accept the fact that the story is to the last degree disjointed, improbable, impossible; lay it aside as a complete failure in what it attempted to be, and read it, as "Vivian Grey" is now read, in the light of the career which it heralded.

A failure as a novel.

Interesting as a self-revelation.

"Morton's Hope" is not to be read as a novel: it is to be studied as an autobiography, a prophecy, a record of aspirations, disguised under a series of incidents which are flung together with no more regard to the unities than a pack of shuffled playing-cards. I can do nothing better than let him picture himself, for it is impossible not to recognize the portrait. It is of little consequence whether every trait is an exact copy from his own features, but it is so obvious that many of the lines are direct transcripts from nature that we may believe the same thing of many others. Let us compare his fictitious hero's story with what we have read of his own life.

Section IV. 1839.

In early boyhood Morton amused himself and astonished those about him by enacting plays for a puppet theatre. This was at six years old, and at twelve we find him acting in a play with other boys, just as Motley's playmates have already described him. The hero may now speak for himself, but we shall all perceive that we are listening to the writer's own story.

"Morton's Hope."

Describes himself.

"I was always a huge reader; my mind was essentially craving and insatiable. Its appetite was enormous, and it devoured too greedily for health. I rejected all guidance in my studies. I already fancied myself a misanthrope. I had taken a step very common for boys of my age, and strove with all my might to be a cynic."

His hunger for knowledge.

He goes on to describe, under the perfectly transparent mask of his hero, the course of his studies. "To poetry, like most infants, I devoted most of my time." From modern poetry he went back to the earlier sources, first with the idea of systematic reading and at last through Chaucer and Gower and early ballads, until he lost himself "in a dismal swamp of barbarous romances and lying Latin chronicles. I got hold of the Bibliotheca Monastica, containing a copious account of Anglo-Norman authors, with notices of their works, and set seriously to reading every one of them." One profit of his antiquarianism, however, was, as he

His study of old authors.

SECTION IV. 1839.

"Morton's Hope."

says, his attention to foreign languages, — French Spanish, German, especially in their earliest and rudest forms of literature. From these he ascended to the ancient poets, and from Latin to Greek. He would have taken up the study of the Oriental languages, but for the advice of a relative, who begged him seriously to turn his attention to history. The paragraph which follows must speak for itself as a true record under a feigned heading.

Describes his own character.

"The groundwork of my early character was plasticity and fickleness. I was mortified by this exposure of my ignorance, and disgusted with my former course of reading. I now set myself violently to the study of history. With my turn of mind, and with the preposterous habits which I had been daily acquiring, I could not fail to make as gross mistakes in the pursuit of this as of other branches of knowledge. I imagined, on setting out, a system of strict and impartial investigation of the sources of history. I was inspired with the absurd ambition, not uncommon to youthful students, of knowing as much as their masters. I imagined it necessary for me, stripling as I was, to study the authorities; and, imbued with the strict necessity of judging for myself, I turned from the limpid pages of the modern historians to the notes and authorities at the bottom of the page. These, of course, sent me back to my monastic acquaintances,

Takes to the study of history.

SECTION IV. 1839.

"Morton's Hope."

and I again found myself in such congenial company to a youthful and ardent mind as Florence of Worcester and Simeon of Durham, the Venerable Bede and Matthew Paris; and so on to Gregory and Fredegarius, down to the more modern and elegant pages of Froissart, Hollinshed, Hooker, and Stowe. Infant as I was, I presumed to grapple with masses of learning almost beyond the strength of the giants of history. A spendthrift of my time and labor, I went out of my way to collect materials, and to build for myself, when I should have known that older and abler architects had already appropriated all that was worth preserving; that the edifice was built, the quarry exhausted, and that I was, consequently, only delving amidst rubbish.

Ill-directed studies.

"This course of study was not absolutely without its advantages. The mind gained a certain proportion of vigor even by this exercise of its faculties, just as my bodily health would have been improved by transporting the refuse ore of a mine from one pit to another, instead of coining the ingots which lay heaped before my eyes. Still, however, my time was squandered. There was a constant want of fitness and concentration of my energies. My dreams of education were boundless, brilliant, indefinite; but alas! they were only dreams. There was nothing accurate and defined in my future course of life. I was ambitious and

Want of concentration.

SECTION IV. 1839.

"Morton's Hope."

conceited, but my aspirations were vague and shapeless. I had crowded together the most gorgeous and even some of the most useful and durable materials for my woof, but I had no pattern, and consequently never began to weave.

Aims at too much.

"I had not made the discovery that an individual cannot learn, nor be, everything; that the world is a factory in which each individual must perform his portion of work: — happy enough if he can choose it according to his taste and talent, but must renounce the desire of observing or superintending the whole operation. . . . .

"From studying and investigating the sources of history with my own eyes, I went a step further; I refused the guidance of modern writers; and proceeding from one point of presumption to another, I came to the magnanimous conviction that I could not know history as I ought to know it unless I *wrote* it for myself. . . . .

Thinks he must *write* history to know it.

"It would be tedious and useless to enlarge upon my various attempts and various failures. I forbear to comment upon mistakes which I was in time wise enough to retrieve. Pushing out as I did, without compass and without experience, on the boundless ocean of learning, what could I expect but an utter and a hopeless shipwreck?

Learned ignorance.

"Thus I went on, becoming more learned, and therefore more ignorant, more confused in my brain, and more awkward in my habits, from day to day. I was ever at my studies, and could hardly be prevailed upon to allot a moment to exercise or recreation. I breakfasted with a pen behind my ear, and dined in company with a folio bigger than the table. I became solitary and morose, the necessary consequence of reckless study; talked impatiently of the value of my time, and the immensity of my labors; spoke contemptuously of the learning and acquirements of the whole world, and threw out mysterious hints of the magnitude and importance of my own projects.

Section IV. 1839.

"Morton's Hope."

Always studying.

Its effects.

"In the midst of all this study and this infant authorship the perusal of such masses of poetry could not fail to produce their effect. Of a youth whose mind, like mine at that period, possessed some general capability, without perhaps a single prominent and marked talent, a proneness to imitation is sure to be the besetting sin. I consequently, for a large portion of my earlier life, never read a work which struck my fancy, without planning a better one upon its model; for my ambition, like my vanity, knew no bounds. It was a matter of course that I should be attacked by the poetic mania. I took the infection at the usual time, went through its various stages, and recovered as soon as could be expected. I discovered soon enough that emulation is not capability, and he is

Poetic mania

SECTION IV. 1839.

"Morton's Hope."

fortunate to whom is soonest revealed the relative extent of his ambition and his powers.

His ambition.

"My ambition was boundless; my dreams of glory were not confined to authorship and literature alone; but every sphere in which the intellect of man exerts itself revolved in a blaze of light before me. And there I sat in my solitude and dreamed such wondrous dreams! Events were thickening around me which were soon to change the world,—but they were unmarked by me. The country was changing to a mighty theatre, on whose stage those who were as great as I fancied myself to be were to enact a stupendous drama in which I had no part. I saw it not; I knew it not; and yet how infinitely beautiful were the imaginations of my solitude! Fancy shook her kaleidoscope each moment as chance directed, and lo! what new, fantastic, brilliant, but what unmeaning visions. My ambitious anticipations were as boundless as they were various and conflicting. There was not a path which leads to glory in which I was not destined to gather laurels. As a warrior I would conquer and overrun the world. As a statesman I would reorganize and govern it. As a historian I would consign it all to immortality; and in my leisure moments I would be a great poet and a man of the world.

Would be and do everything.

"In short, I was already enrolled in that large category of what are called young men of genius,—

"Morton's Hope."

men who are the pride of their sisters and the glory of their grandmothers, — men of whom unheard-of things are expected, till after long preparation comes a portentous failure, and then they are forgotten; subsiding into indifferent apprentices and attorneys' clerks.

Disappointed expectations.

"Alas for the golden imaginations of our youth! They are bright and beautiful, but they fade. They glitter brightly enough to deceive the wisest and most cautious, and we garner them up in the most secret caskets of our hearts; but are they not like the coins which the Dervise gave the merchant in the story? When we look for them the next morning, do we not find them withered leaves?"

His hero's story is his own.

The ideal picture just drawn is only a fuller portraiture of the youth whose outlines have been already sketched by the companions of his earlier years. If his hero says, "I breakfasted with a pen behind my ear and dined in company with a folio bigger than the table," one of his family says of the boy Motley that "if there were five minutes before dinner, when he came into the parlor he always took up some book near at hand and began to read until dinner was announced." The same unbounded thirst for knowledge, the same history of various attempts and various failures, the same ambition, not yet fixed in its aim, but showing itself in rest-

SECTION IV. 1839.

less effort, belong to the hero of the story and its narrator.

"Morton's Hope."

First attempts not to be undervalued.

Let no man despise the first efforts of immature genius. Nothing can be more crude as a novel, nothing more disappointing, than "Morton's Hope." But in no other of Motley's writings do we get such an inside view of his character with its varied impulses, its capricious appetites, its unregulated forces, its impatient grasp for all kinds of knowledge. With all his university experiences at home and abroad, it might be said with a large measure of truth that he was a self-educated man, as he had been a self-taught boy. His instincts were too powerful to let him work quietly in the common round of school and college training. Looking at him as his companions describe him, as he delineates himself *mutato nomine*, the chances of success would have seemed to all but truly prophetic eyes very doubtful, if not decidedly against him. Too many brilliant young novel-readers and lovers of poetry, excused by their admirers for their shortcomings on the strength of their supposed birthright of "genius," have ended where they began; flattered into the vain belief that they were men at eighteen or twenty, and finding out at fifty that they were and always had been nothing more than boys. It was but a tangled skein of life that Motley's book showed us at twenty-five, and older men might

"Morton's Hope."

well have doubted whether it would ever be wound off in any continuous thread. To repeat his own words, he had crowded together the materials for his work, but he had no pattern, and consequently never began to weave.

The more this first work of Motley's is examined, the more are its faults as a story and its interest as a self-revelation made manifest to the reader. The future historian, who spared no pains to be accurate, falls into the most extraordinary anachronisms in almost every chapter. Brutus in a bob-wig, Othello in a swallow-tail coat, could hardly be more incongruously equipped than some of his characters in the manner of thought, the phrases, the way of bearing themselves which belong to them in the tale, but never could have belonged to characters of our Revolutionary period. He goes so far in his carelessness as to mix up dates in such a way as almost to convince us that he never looked over his own manuscript or proofs. His hero is in Prague in June, 1777, reading a letter received from America in less than a fortnight from the date of its being written; in August of the same year he is in the American camp, where he is found in the company of a certain Colonel Waldron, an officer of some standing in the Revolutionary Army, with whom he is said to have been constantly associated for some three months, having arrived in

Anachronisms in his novel.

SECTION IV. 1839.

"Morton's Hope."

America, as he says, on the 15th of May, that is to say, six weeks or more before he sailed, according to his previous account. Bohemia seems to have bewitched his chronology as it did Shakespeare's geography. To have made his story a consistent series of contradictions, Morton should have sailed from that Bohemian seashore which may be found in "A Winter's Tale," but not in the map of Europe.

Redeeming passages.

And yet in the midst of all these marks of haste and negligence, here and there the philosophical student of history betrays himself, the ideal of noble achievement glows in an eloquent paragraph, or is embodied in a loving portrait like that of the professor and historian Harlem. The novel, taken in connection with the subsequent developments of the writer's mind, is a study of singular interest. It is a chaos before the creative epoch; the light has not been divided from the darkness; the firmament has not yet divided the waters from the waters. The forces at work in a human intelligence to bring harmony out of its discordant movements are as mysterious, as miraculous, we might truly say, as those which give shape and order to the confused materials out of which habitable worlds are evolved. It is too late now to be sensitive over this unsuccessful attempt as a story and unconscious success as a self-portraiture. The first sketches of Paul

"Morton's Hope."

Veronese, the first patterns of the Gobelin tapestry, are not to be criticised for the sake of pointing out their inevitable and too manifest imperfections. They are to be carefully studied as the earliest efforts of the hand which painted the Marriage at Cana, of the art which taught the rude fabrics made to be trodden under foot to rival the glowing canvas of the great painters. None of Motley's subsequent writings give such an insight into his character and mental history. It took many years to train the as yet undisciplined powers into orderly obedience, and to bring the unarranged materials into the organic connection which was needed in the construction of a work that should endure. There was a long interval between his early manhood and the middle term of life, during which the slow process of evolution was going on. There are plants which open their flowers with the first rays of the sun; there are others that wait until evening to spread their petals. It was already the high noon of life with him before his genius had truly shown itself; if he had not lived beyond this period he would have left nothing to give him a lasting name.

V.

First Diplomatic Appointment, — Secretary of Legation to the Russian Mission. — Brief Residence at St. Petersburg. — Letter to his Mother. — Return. (1841 - 1842.)

SECTION V.
1841 - 1842.

First diplomatic appointment.

IN the autumn of 1841 Mr. Motley received the appointment of Secretary of Legation to the Russian Mission, Mr. Todd being then the Minister. Arriving at St. Petersburg just at the beginning of winter, he found the climate acting very unfavorably upon his spirits if not upon his health, and was unwilling that his wife and his two young children should be exposed to its rigors. The expense of living, also, was out of proportion to his income, and his letters show that he had hardly established himself in St. Petersburg before he had made up his mind to leave a place where he found he had nothing to do and little to enjoy. He was homesick, too, as a young husband and father with an affectionate nature like his ought to have been under these circumstances. He did not regret having made the experiment, for he knew that he should not have been satisfied with himself if he had not made it. It was his first trial of a career in which he contemplated embarking, and in which afterwards he had an eventful experience. In his private letters to his family, many of which I have had the privilege of looking over, he mentions in detail all the reasons which influenced him in forming his own opinion about the expediency of a continued residence at St. Petersburg, and leaves the decision to her in whose judgment he always had the greatest confidence. No unpleasant circumstance attended his resignation of his Secretaryship, and though it must have been a disappointment to find that the place did not suit him, as he and his family were then situated, it was only at the worst an experiment fairly tried and not proving satisfactory. He left St. Petersburg after a few months' residence, and returned to America. On reaching New York he was met by the sad tidings of the death of his first-born child, a boy of great promise, who had called out all the affections of his ardent nature. It was long before he recovered from the shock of this great affliction. The boy had shown a very quick and bright intelligence, and his father often betrayed a pride in his gifts and graces which he never for a moment made apparent in regard to his own.

Resigns and returns to America.

Death of his son.

Among the letters which he wrote from St. Petersburg are two miniature ones directed to this little boy. His affectionate disposition shows itself very sweetly in these touching mementos of a love of which his first great sorrow was so soon to be born. Not less charming are his letters to his mother, showing the tenderness with which he always regarded her, and full of all the details which he thought would entertain one to whom all that related to her children was always interesting. Of the letters to his wife it is needless to say more than that they always show the depth of the love he bore her and the absolute trust he placed in her, consulting her at all times as his nearest and wisest friend and adviser, — one in all respects fitted

His letters.

To warn, to comfort, and command.

I extract a passage from one of his letters to his mother, as much for the sake of lending a character of reality to his brief residence at St. Petersburg as for that of the pleasant picture it gives us of an interior in that Northern capital.

From a letter to his mother.

"We entered through a small vestibule, with the usual arrangement of treble doors, padded with leather to exclude the cold, and guarded by two 'proud young porters' in severe cocked hats and formidable batons, into a broad hall, — threw off our furred boots and cloaks, ascended a carpeted marble staircase, in every angle of which stood a statuesque footman in gaudy coat and unblemished unmentionables, and reached a broad land-

Description of a Russian interior.

ing upon the top thronged as usual with servants. Thence we passed through an antechamber into a long, high, brilliantly lighted, saffron-papered room, in which a dozen card-tables were arranged, and thence into the receiving-room. This was a large room, with a splendidly inlaid and polished floor, the walls covered with crimson satin, the cornices heavily incrusted with gold, and the ceiling beautifully painted in arabesque. The massive fauteuils and sofas, as also the drapery, were of crimson satin with a profusion of gilding. The ubiquitous portrait of the Emperor was the only picture, and was the same you see everywhere. This crimson room had the doors upon the side facing the three windows. The innermost opened into a large supper-room, in which a table was spread covered with the usual refreshments of European parties, — tea, ices, lemonade, and et ceteras, — and the other opened into a ball-room which is a sort of miniature of the 'salle blanche' of the Winter Palace, being white and gold, and very brilliantly lighted with 'ormolu' chandeliers filled with myriads of candles. This room (at least forty feet long by perhaps twenty-five) opened into a carpeted conservatory of about the same size, filled with orange-trees and japonica plants covered with fruit and flowers, arranged very gracefully into arbors, with luxurious seats under the pendent boughs, and with here and there a pretty marble statue gleaming through the green and glossy leaves. One might almost have imagined one's self in the 'land of the cypress and myrtle' instead of our actual whereabout upon the polar banks of the Neva. Wandering through these mimic groves or reposing from the fatigues of the dance, was many a fair and graceful form, while the brilliantly lighted ball-room, filled with hundreds of exquisitely dressed women (for the Russian ladies, if not very pretty, are graceful, and make admirable toilettes), formed a dazzling contrast with the tempered light of the 'Winter Garden.' The conservatory opened into a library, and from the library you reach the antechamber, thus completing the 'giro' of one of the prettiest houses in St. Petersburg. I waltzed one waltz and quadrilled one quadrille — but it was hard work — and as the sole occupation of these parties is dancing and card-playing — conversation apparently not being customary — they are to me not very attractive."

Russian ladies.

He could not be happy alone, and there were good reasons against his being joined by his wife and children.

"With my reserved habits," he says, "it would take a great deal longer to become intimate here than to thaw the Baltic. I have only to 'knock that it shall be opened to me,' but that is just what

I hate to do. . . . . 'Man delights not me, no, nor woman neither.' "

His return.

Disappointed in his expectations, but happy in the thought of meeting his wife and children, he came back to his household to find it clad in mourning for the loss of its first-born.

His bereavement.

VI.

Letter to Park Benjamin. — Political Views and Feelings. (1844.)

Section VI. 1844.

Letter to Mr. Park Benjamin.

A letter to Mr. Park Benjamin, dated December 17, 1844, which has been kindly lent me by Mrs. Mary Lanman Douw of Poughkeepsie, gives a very complete and spirited account of himself at this period. He begins with a quiet, but tender reference to the death of his younger brother, Preble, one of the most beautiful youths seen or remembered among us, "a great favorite," as he says, "in the family and indeed with every one who knew him." He mentions the fact that his friends and near connections, the Stackpoles, are in Washington, which place he considers as exceptionably odious at the time when he is writing. The election of Mr. Polk as the opponent of Henry Clay gives him a discouraged feeling about our institutions. The question, he thinks, is now settled that a *statesman* can never again be called to administer the government of the country. He is almost if not quite in despair "because it is now proved that a man, take him for all in all, better qualified by

Election of Mr. Polk.

Letter to Mr. Park Benjamin.

intellectual power, energy and purity of character, knowledge of men, a great combination of personal qualities, a frank, high-spirited, manly bearing, keen sense of honor, the power of attracting and winning men, united with a vast experience in affairs, such as no man (but John Quincy Adams) now living has had and no man in this country can ever have again,— I say it is proved that a man better qualified by an extraordinary combination of advantages to administer the government than any man now living, or any man we can ever produce again, can be beaten by anybody. . . . . It has taken forty years of public life to prepare such a man for the Presidency, and the result is that he can be beaten by anybody — Mr. Polk is anybody — he is Mr. Quelconque."

I do not venture to quote the most burning sentences of this impassioned letter. It shows that Motley had not only become interested most profoundly in the general movements of parties, but that he had followed the course of political events which resulted in the election of Mr. Polk with careful study, and that he was already looking forward to the revolt of the slave States which occurred fifteen years later. The letter is full of fiery eloquence, now and then extravagant and even violent in expression, but throbbing with a generous heat which shows the excitable spirit of

Section VI. 1844.

Letter to Mr. Park Benjamin.

a man who wishes to be proud of his country and does not wish to keep his temper when its acts make him ashamed of it. He is disgusted and indignant to the last degree at seeing "Mr. Quelconque" chosen over the illustrious statesman who was his favorite candidate. But all his indignation cannot repress a sense of humor which was one of his marked characteristics. After fatiguing his vocabulary with hard usage, after his unsparing denunciation of "the very dirty politics" which he finds mixed up with our popular institutions, he says, — it must be remembered that this was an offhand letter to one nearly connected with him, — "All these things must in short, to use the energetic language of the Balm of Columbia advertisement, 'bring every generous thinking youth to that heavy sinking gloom which not even the loss of property can produce, but only the loss of hair, which brings on premature decay, causing many to shrink from being uncovered, and even to shun society, to avoid the jests and sneers of their acquaintances. The remainder of their lives is consequently spent in retirement.'"

He continues: "Before dropping the subject, and to show the perfect purity of my motives, I will add that I am not at all anxious about the legislation of the new government. I desired the election of Clay as a moral triumph, and because

Letter to Mr. Park Benjamin.

the *administration* of the country, at this moment of ten thousand times more importance than its legislation, would have been placed in pure, strong, and determined hands."

Then comes a dash of that satirical and somewhat cynical way of feeling which he had not as yet outgrown. He had been speaking about the general want of attachment to the Union and the absence of the sentiment of loyalty as bearing on the probable dissolution of the Union.

"I don't mean to express any opinions on these matters — I have n't got any. It seems to me that the best way is to look at the hodge-podge, be good-natured if possible, and laugh,

> As from the height of contemplation
> We view the feeble joints men totter on.

I began a tremendous political career during the election, having made two stump speeches of an hour and a half each, — after you went away, — one in Dedham town-hall and one in Jamaica Plain, with such eminent success that many invitations came to me from the surrounding villages, and if I had continued in active political life I might have risen to be vote-distributor, or fence-viewer, or selectman, or hog-reeve, or something of the kind."

The letter from which the above passages are

SECTION VI. 1844.

Letter to Mr. Park Benjamin.

quoted gives the same portrait of the writer, only seen in profile, as it were, which we have already seen drawn in full face in the story of "Morton's Hope." It is charged with that *sæva indignatio* which at times verges on misanthropic contempt for its objects, not unnatural to a high-spirited young man who sees his lofty ideals confronted with the ignoble facts which strew the highways of political life. But we can recognize real conviction and the deepest feeling beneath his scornful rhetoric and his bitter laugh. He was no more a mere *dilettante* than Swift himself, but now and then in the midst of his most serious thought some absurd or grotesque image will obtrude itself, and one is reminded of the lines on the monument of Gay rather than of the fierce epitaph of the Dean of Saint Patrick's.

VII.

First Historical and Critical Essays. — Peter the Great. — Novels of Balzac. — Polity of the Puritans. (*1845-1847.*)

SECT. VII. 1845.

Essay in the N. A. Review.

Peter the Great.

MR. MOTLEY'S first serious effort in historical composition was an article of fifty pages in the North American Review for October, 1845. This was nominally a notice of two works, one on Russia, the other A Memoir of the Life of Peter the Great. It is however a narrative rather than a criticism, a rapid, continuous, brilliant, almost dramatic narrative. If there had been any question as to whether the young novelist who had missed his first mark had in him the elements which might give him success as an author, this essay would have settled the question. It shows throughout that the writer has made a thorough study of his subject, but it is written with an easy and abundant, yet scholarly freedom, not as if he were surrounded by his authorities and picking out his material piece by piece, but rather as if it were the overflow of long-pursued and well-remembered studies recalled without effort and poured forth almost as a recreation.

SECT. VII. 1845.

Essay; Peter the Great.

As he betrayed or revealed his personality in his first novel, so in this first effort in another department of literature he showed in epitome his qualities as a historian and a biographer. The hero of his narrative makes his entrance at once in his character as the shipwright of Saardam, on the occasion of a visit of the great Duke of Marlborough. The portrait instantly arrests attention. His ideal personages had been drawn in such a sketchy way, they presented so many imperfectly harmonized features, that they never became real, with the exception of course of the story-teller himself. But the vigor with which the presentment of the imperial ship-carpenter, the sturdy, savage, eager, fiery Peter, was given in the few opening sentences, showed the movement of the hand, the glow of the color, that were in due time to display on a broader canvas the full-length portraits of William the Silent and of John of Barneveld. The style of the whole article is rich, fluent, picturesque, with light touches of humor here and there, and perhaps a trace or two of youthful jauntiness, not quite as yet outgrown. His illustrative poetical quotations are mostly from Shakespeare, — from Milton and Byron also in a passage or two, — and now and then one is reminded that he is not unfamiliar with Carlyle's Sartor Resartus and the French Revolution of the same unmistakable writer, more per-

Style of this article.

haps by the way in which phrases borrowed from other authorities are set in the text than by any more important evidence of unconscious imitation.

His Essay applauded.

The readers who had shaken their heads over the unsuccessful story of "Morton's Hope" were startled by the appearance of this manly and scholarly essay. This young man, it seemed, had been studying, — studying with careful accuracy, with broad purpose. He could paint a character with the ruddy life-blood coloring it as warmly as it glows in the cheeks of one of Van der Helst's burgomasters. He could sweep the horizon in a wide general outlook, and manage his perspective and his lights and shadows so as to place and accent his special subject with its due relief and just relations. It was a sketch, or rather a study for a larger picture, but it betrayed the hand of a master. The feeling of many was that expressed in the words of Mr. Longfellow in his review of the "Twice-Told Tales" of the unknown young writer, Nathaniel Hawthorne: "When a new star rises in the heavens, people gaze after it for a season with the naked eye, and with such telescopes as they may find. . . . . This star is but newly risen; and erelong the observation of numerous star-gazers, perched up on arm-chairs and editor's tables, will inform the world of its magnitude and its place in the heaven of" —

not poetry in this instance, but that serene and unclouded region of the firmament where shine unchanging the names of Herodotus and Thucidydes. Those who had always believed in their brilliant schoolmate and friend at last felt themselves justified in their faith. The artist that sent this unframed picture to be hung in a corner of the literary gallery was equal to larger tasks. There was but one voice in the circle that surrounded the young Essayist. He must redeem his pledge, he can and will redeem it, if he will only follow the bent of his genius and grapple with the heroic labor of writing a great history.

And this was the achievement he was already meditating.

Critical Essay on Balzac.

In the mean time he was studying history for its facts and principles, and fiction for its scenery and portraits. In the North American Review for July, 1847, is a long and characteristic article on Balzac, of whom he was an admirer, but with no blind worship. The readers of this great story-teller, who was so long in obtaining recognition, who "made twenty assaults upon fame and had forty books killed under him" before he achieved success, will find his genius fully appreciated and fairly weighed in this discriminating essay. A few brief extracts will show its quality.

"Balzac is an artist, and only an artist. In his

Sect. VII. 1847.

Criticism of Balzac.

tranquil, unimpassioned, remorseless diagnosis of morbid phenomena, in his cool method of treating the morbid anatomy of the heart, in his curiously accurate dissection of the passions, in the patient and painful attention with which, stethoscope in hand, finger on pulse, eye everywhere, you see him watching every symptom, alive to every sound and every breath, and in the scientific accuracy with which he portrays the phenomena which have been the subject of his investigation, — in all this calm and conscientious study of nature he often reminds us of Goethe. Balzac, however, is only an artist. . . . . He is neither moral nor immoral, but a calm and profound observer of human society and human passions, and a minute, patient, and powerful delineator of scenes and characters in the world before his eyes. His readers must moralize for themselves. . . . . It is, perhaps, his defective style more than anything else which will prevent his becoming a classic, for style above all other qualities seems to embalm for posterity. As for his philosophy, his principles, moral, political, or social, we repeat that he seems to have none whatever. He looks for the picturesque and the striking. He studies sentiments and sensations from an artistic point of view. He is a physiognomist, a physiologist, a bit of an anatomist, a bit of a mesmerist, a bit of a geologist, a Flemish painter, an upholsterer,

Sect. VII. 1849.

a micrological, misanthropical, sceptical philosopher; but he is no moralist, and certainly no reformer."

Essay; "Polity of the Puritans."

Another article contributed by Mr. Motley to the North American Review is to be found in the number for October, 1849. It is nominally a review of Talvi's (Mrs. Robinson's) Geschicht der Colonisation von New England, but in reality an essay on the "Polity of the Puritans," — an historical disquisition on the principles of self-government evolved in New England, broad in its views, eloquent in its language. Its spirit is thoroughly American, and its estimate of the Puritan character is not narrowed by the near-sighted liberalism which sees the past in the pitiless light of the present, — which looks around at high noon and finds fault with early dawn for its long and dark shadows. Here is a sentence or two from the article: —

"With all the faults of the system devised by the Puritans, it was a practical system. With all their foibles, with all their teasing, tyrannical, and arbitrary notions, the Pilgrims were lovers of liberty as well as sticklers for authority. . . . Nowhere can a better description of liberty be found than that given by Winthrop, in his defence of himself before the General Court on a charge of arbitrary conduct. 'Nor would I have you mistake your

Essay; "Polity of the Puritans."

own liberty,' he says. 'There is a freedom of doing what we list, without regard to law or justice; this liberty is indeed inconsistent with authority; but civil, moral, and federal liberty consists in every man's enjoying his property and having the benefit of the laws of his country; which is very consistent with a due subjection to the civil magistrate.' . . . .

"We enjoy an inestimable advantage in America. One can be a republican, a democrat, without being a radical. A *radical,* one who would *uproot,* is a man whose trade is dangerous to society. Here is but little to uproot. The trade cannot flourish. All classes are conservative by necessity, for none can wish to change the structure of our polity. . . . .

"The country without a past cannot be intoxicated by visions of the past of other lands. Upon this absence of the past it seems to us that much of the security of our institutions depends. Nothing interferes with the development of what is now felt to be the true principle of government, the will of the people legitimately expressed. To establish that great truth, nothing was to be torn down, nothing to be uprooted. It grew up in New England out of the seed unconsciously planted by the first Pilgrims, was not crushed out by the weight of a thousand years of error spread over the whole continent, and the Revolution was proclaimed and recognized."

VIII.

Joseph Lewis Stackpole, the friend of Motley. His sudden death.— Motley in the Massachusetts House of Representatives. — Second Novel, — "Merry-Mount, A Romance of the Massachusetts Colony." (1847-1849.)

SECT. VIII. 1847.

THE intimate friendships of early manhood are not very often kept up among our people. The eager pursuit of fortune, position, office, separates young friends, and the indoor home life imprisons them in the domestic circle so generally that it is quite exceptional to find two grown men who are like brothers, — or rather unlike most brothers, in being constantly found together. An exceptional instance of such a more than fraternal relation was seen in the friendship of Mr. Motley and Mr. Joseph Lewis Stackpole. Mr. William Amory, who knew them both well, has kindly furnished me with some recollections, which I cannot improve by changing his own language.

Friendship with J. L. Stackpole.

"Their intimacy began in Europe, and they returned to this country in 1835. In 1837 they married sisters, and this cemented their intimacy, which continued to Stackpole's death in 1847. The contrast in the temperament of the two friends — the one sensitive and irritable, and the other always cool and good-natured — only increased their mutual attachment to each other, and Motley's dependence upon Stackpole. Never were two friends more constantly together or more affectionately fond of each other. As Stackpole was about eight years older than Motley, and much less impulsive and more discreet, his death was to his friend irreparable, and at the time an overwhelming blow."

Mr. Stackpole was a man of great intelligence, of remarkable personal attractions, and amiable character. His death was a loss to Motley even greater than he knew, for he needed just such a friend, older, calmer, more experienced in the ways of the world, and above all capable of thoroughly understanding him and exercising a wholesome influence over his excitable nature without the seeming of a Mentor preaching to a Telemachus. Mr. Stackpole was killed by a railroad accident on the 20th of July, 1847.

Death of J. L. Stackpole.

In the same letter Mr. Amory refers to a very different experience in Mr. Motley's life, — his one year of service as a member of the Massachusetts House of Representatives, 1849.

"In respect to the one term during which he

SECT. VIII. 1849.

was a member of the Massachusetts House of Representatives, I can recall only one thing, to which he often and laughingly alluded. Motley, as the Chairman of the Committee on Education, made, as he thought, a most masterly Report. It was very elaborate, and, as he supposed, unanswerable; but Boutwell, then a young man from some country town [Groton, Mass.], rose, and as Motley always said, demolished the Report, so that he was unable to defend it against the attack. You can imagine his disgust, after the pains he had taken to render it unassailable, to find himself, as he expressed it, 'on his own dunghill,' ignominiously beaten. While the result exalted his opinion of the speech-making faculty of a Representative of a common school education, it at the same time cured him of any ambition for political promotion in Massachusetts."

Mr. Motley in the Mass. H. of Representatives.

His Report on Education.

To my letter of inquiry about this matter, Hon. George S. Boutwell courteously returned the following answer: —

BOSTON, October 14, 1878.

Mr. Boutwell's letter.

MY DEAR SIR, — As my memory serves me, Mr. Motley was a member of the Massachusetts House of Representatives in the year 1847 [1849]. It may be well to consult the Manual for that year. I recollect the controversy over the Report from the Committee on Education.

His failure was not due to his want of faculty or to the vigor of his opponents.

His Report on Education.

In truth he espoused the weak side of the question and the unpopular one also. His proposition was to endow the colleges at the expense of the fund for the support of the common schools. Failure was inevitable. Neither Webster nor Choate could have carried the bill.

Very truly,

GEO. S. BOUTWELL.

He accepts its failure cheerfully.

No one could be more ready and willing to recognize his own failures than Motley. He was as honest and manly, perhaps I may say as sympathetic with the feeling of those about him, on this occasion, as was Charles Lamb, who, sitting with his sister in the front of the pit, on the night when his farce was damned at its first representation, gave way to the common feeling, and hissed and hooted lustily with the others around him. It was what might be expected from his honest and truthful nature, sometimes too severe in judging itself.

The commendation bestowed upon Motley's historical Essays in the North American Review must have gone far towards compensating him for the ill success of his earlier venture. It pointed clearly towards the field in which he was to gather his laurels. And it was in the year following the pub-

SECT. VIII. 1849.

lication of the first Essay, or about that time (1846), that he began collecting materials for a history of Holland.

Whether to tell the story of men that have lived and of events that have happened, or to create the characters and invent the incidents of an imaginary tale be the higher task, we need not stop to discuss. But the young author was just now like the great actor in Sir Joshua's picture, between the allurements of Thalia and Melpomene, still doubtful whether he was to be a romancer or a historian.

His second novel, "Merry-Mount."

The tale of which the title is given at the beginning of this section had been written several years before the date of its publication. It is a great advance in certain respects over the first novel, but wants the peculiar interest which belonged to that as a partially autobiographical memoir. The story is no longer disjointed and impossible. It is carefully studied in regard to its main facts. It has less to remind us of "Vivian Grey" and "Pelham," and more that recalls "Woodstock" and "Kenilworth." The personages were many of them historical, though idealized; the occurrences were many of them such as the record authenticated; the localities were drawn largely from nature. The story betrays marks of haste or carelessness in some portions, though others are elaborately studied. His preface shows that the reception of his first book had made him timid and sensitive about the fate of the second, and explains and excuses what might be found fault with, to disarm the criticism he had some reason to fear.

His second novel, "Merry Mount."

That old watch-dog of our American literature, the North American Review, always ready with lambent phrases in stately "Articles" for native talent of a certain pretension, and wagging its appendix of "Critical Notices" kindly at the advent of humbler merit, treated "Merry-Mount" with the distinction implied in a review of nearly twenty pages. This was a great contrast to the brief and slighting notice of "Morton's Hope." The reviewer thinks the author's descriptive power wholly exceeds his conception of character and invention of circumstances. "He dwells, perhaps, too long and fondly upon his imagination of the landscape as it was before the stillness of the forest had been broken by the axe of the settler; but the picture is so finely drawn, with so much beauty of language and purity of sentiment, that we cannot blame him for lingering upon the scene. . . . . The story is not managed with much skill, but it has variety enough of incident and character, and is told with so much liveliness that few will be inclined to lay it down before reaching the conclusion. . . . . The writer certainly needs practice in elaborating the details of a consistent and interesting novel; but in many respects

Criticisms upon it.

SECT. VIII. 1849.

he is well qualified for the task, and we shall be glad to meet him again on the half-historical ground he has chosen. His present work, certainly, is not a fair specimen of what he is able to accomplish, and its failure, or partial success, ought only to inspirit him for further effort."

Still collecting materials for a history.

The "half-historical ground" he had chosen had already led him to the entrance into the broader domain of history. The "further effort" for which he was to be inspirited had already begun. He had been for some time, as was before mentioned, collecting materials for the work which was to cast all his former attempts into the kindly shadow of oblivion save when from time to time the light of his brilliant after success is thrown upon them to illustrate the path by which it was at length attained.

IX.

Plan of a History.—Letters. (*1850.*)

SECTION IX.
1850.

THE reputation of Mr. Prescott was now coextensive with the realm of scholarship. The Histories of the reign of Ferdinand and Isabella and of the Conquest of Mexico had met with a reception which might well tempt the ambition of a young writer to emulate it, but which was not likely to be awarded to any second candidate who should enter the field in rivalry with the great and universally popular historian. But this was the field on which Mr. Motley was to venture.

Relations with Mr. Prescott.

After he had chosen the subject of the history he contemplated, he found that Mr. Prescott was occupied with a kindred one, so that there might be too near a coincidence between them. I must borrow from Mr. Ticknor's beautiful Life of Prescott the words which introduce a letter of Motley's to Mr. William Amory, who has kindly allowed me also to make use of it.

"The moment, therefore, that he [Mr. Motley] was aware of this condition of things, and the consequent possibility that there might be an untoward interference in their plans, he took the same frank

SECTION IX. 1850.

and honorable course with Mr. Prescott that Mr. Prescott had taken in relation to Mr. Irving, when he found that they had both been contemplating a 'History of the Conquest of Mexico.' The result was the same. Mr. Prescott, instead of treating the matter as an interference, earnestly encouraged Mr. Motley to go on, and placed at his disposition such of the books in his library as could be most useful to him. How amply and promptly he did it, Mr. Motley's own account will best show. It is in a letter dated at Rome, 26th February, 1859, the day he heard of Mr. Prescott's death, and was addressed to his intimate friend, Mr. William Amory, of Boston, Mr. Prescott's much loved brother-in-law."

Mr. Prescott encourages him.

"It seems to me but as yesterday," Mr. Motley writes, "though it must be now twelve years ago, that I was talking with our ever-lamented friend Stackpole about my intention of writing a history upon a subject to which I have since that time been devoting myself. I had then made already some general studies in reference to it, without being in the least aware that Prescott had the intention of writing the 'History of Philip the Second.' Stackpole had heard the fact, and that large preparations had already been made for the work, although 'Peru' had not yet been published. I felt naturally much disappointed. I was conscious

Mr. Motley's letter to Mr. William Amory.

of the immense disadvantage to myself of making my appearance, probably at the same time, before the public, with a work not at all similar in plan to Philip the Second, but which must of necessity traverse a portion of the same ground.

Letter to Mr. Amory.

"My first thought was inevitably, as it were, only of myself. It seemed to me that I had nothing to do but to abandon at once a cherished dream, and probably to renounce authorship. For I had not first made up my mind to write a history, and then cast about to take up a subject. My subject had taken me up, drawn me on, and absorbed me into itself. It was necessary for me, it seemed, to write the book I had been thinking much of, even if it were destined to fall dead from the press, and I had no inclination or interest to write any other. When I had made up my mind accordingly, it then occurred to me that Prescott might not be pleased that I should come forward upon his ground. It is true that no announcement of his intentions had been made, and that he had not, I believe, even commenced his preliminary studies for Philip. At the same time I thought it would be disloyal on my part not to go to him at once, confer with him on the subject, and if I should find a shadow of dissatisfaction on his mind at my proposition, to abandon my plan altogether.

"I had only the slightest acquaintance with him

Section IX. 1850.

Letter to Mr. Amory.

at that time. I was comparatively a young man, and certainly not entitled on any ground to more than the common courtesy which Prescott never could refuse to any one. But he received me with such a frank and ready and liberal sympathy, and such an open-hearted, guileless expansiveness, that I felt a personal affection for him from that hour. I remember the interview as if it had taken place yesterday. It was in his father's house, in his own library, looking on the garden-house and garden, — honored father and illustrious son, — alas! all numbered with the things that were! He assured me that he had not the slightest objection whatever to my plan, that he wished me every success, and that, if there were any books in his library bearing on my subject that I liked to use, they were entirely at my service. After I had expressed my gratitude for his kindness and cordiality, by which I had been in a very few moments set completely at ease, — so far as my fears of his disapprobation went, — I also very naturally stated my opinion that the danger was entirely mine, and that it was rather wilful of me thus to risk such a collision at my first venture, the probable consequence of which was utter shipwreck. I recollect how kindly and warmly he combated this opinion, assuring me that no two books, as he said, ever injured each other, and encouraging me in the warmest and most ear-

Mr. Prescott's generous conduct.

nest manner to proceed on the course I had marked out for myself.

Letter to Mr. Amory.

"Had the result of that interview been different, — had he distinctly stated, or even vaguely hinted, that it would be as well if I should select some other topic, or had he only sprinkled me with the cold water of conventional and commonplace encouragement, — I should have gone from him with a chill upon my mind, and, no doubt, have laid down the pen at once; for, as I have already said, it was not that I cared about writing a history, but that I felt an inevitable impulse to write *one particular history.*

Mr. Prescott's kindness.

"You know how kindly he always spoke of and to me; and the generous manner in which, without the slightest hint from me, and entirely unexpected by me, he attracted the eyes of his hosts of readers to my forthcoming work, by so handsomely alluding to it in the Preface to his own, must be almost as fresh in your memory as it is in mine.

"And although it seems easy enough for a man of world-wide reputation thus to extend the right hand of fellowship to an unknown and struggling aspirant, yet I fear that the history of literature will show that such instances of disinterested kindness are as rare as they are noble."

It was not from any feeling that Mr. Motley was

SECTION IX. 1850.

Mr. Prescott recognizes Mr. Motley's force as a competitor.

a young writer from whose rivalry he had nothing to apprehend. Mr. Amory says that Prescott expressed himself very decidedly to the effect that an author who had written such descriptive passages as were to be found in Mr. Motley's published writings was not to be undervalued as a competitor by any one. The reader who will turn to the description of Charles River in the eighth chapter of the second volume of "Merry Mount," or of the autumnal woods in the sixteenth chapter of the same volume, will see good reason for Mr. Prescott's appreciation of the force of the rival whose advent he so heartily and generously welcomed.

X.

Historical Studies in Europe. — Letter from Brussels.
(*1851 - 1856.*)

SECTION X.
1851 - 1856.

AFTER working for several years on his projected History of the Dutch Republic, he found that, in order to do justice to his subject, he must have recourse to the authorities to be found only in the libraries and state archives of Europe. In the year 1851 he left America with his family, to begin his task over again, throwing aside all that he had already done, and following up his new course of investigations at Berlin, Dresden, the Hague, and Brussels during several succeeding years. I do not know that I can give a better idea of his mode of life during this busy period, his occupations, his state of mind, his objects of interest outside of his special work, than by making the following extracts from a long letter to myself, dated Brussels, 20th November, 1853.

Visits Europe to study for his work.

After some personal matters he continues : —

Writes from Brussels.

"I don't really know what to say to you. I am in a town which, for aught I know, may be very gay. I don't know a living soul in it. We have

SECTION X. 1853.

Letter from Brussels.

not a single acquaintance in the place, and we glory in the fact. There is something rather sublime in thus floating on a single spar in the wide sea of a populous, busy, fuming, fussy world like this. At any rate it is consonant to both our tastes. You may suppose, however, that I find it rather difficult to amuse my friends out of the incidents of so isolated an existence. Our daily career is very regular and monotonous. Our life is as stagnant as a Dutch canal. Not that I complain of it, — on the contrary, the canal may be richly freighted with merchandise and be a short cut to the ocean of abundant and perpetual knowledge; but, at the same time, few points rise above the level of so regular a life, to be worthy of your notice. You must, therefore, allow me to meander along the meadows of commonplace. Don't expect anything of the impetuous and boiling style. We go it weak here. I don't know whether you were ever in Brussels. It is a striking, picturesque town, built up a steep promontory, the old part at the bottom, very dingy and mouldy, the new part at the top, very showy and elegant. Nothing can be more exquisite in its way than the *grande place* in the very heart of the city, surrounded with those toppling, zigzag, ten-storied buildings bedizened all over with ornaments and emblems so peculiar to the Netherlands, with the brocaded Hotel de Ville on

Section X. 1853.

Letter from Brussels.

one side, with its impossible spire rising some three hundred and seventy feet into the air and embroidered to the top with the delicacy of needle-work, sugar-work, spider-work, or what you will. I haunt this place because it is my scene, — my theatre. Here were enacted so many deep tragedies, so many stately dramas, and even so many farces, which have been familiar to me so long that I have got to imagine myself invested with a kind of property in the place, and look at it as if it were merely the theatre with the coulisses, machinery, drapery, etc., for representing scenes which have long since vanished, and which no more enter the minds of the men and women who are actually moving across its pavements than if they had occurred in the moon. When I say that I knew no soul in Brussels I am perhaps wrong. With the present generation I am not familiar. *En revanche,* the dead men of the place are my intimate friends. I am at home in any cemetery. With the fellows of the sixteenth century I am on the most familiar terms. Any ghost that ever flits by night across the moonlight square is at once hailed by me as a man and a brother. I call him by his Christian name at once. When you come out of this place, however, which, as I said, is in the heart of the town — the antique gem in the modern setting — you may go either up or down — if you go

Section X. 1853.

Letter from Brussels.

down you will find yourself in the very nastiest complications of lanes and culs-de-sacs possible — a dark entanglement of gin-shops, beer-houses, and hovels, — through which charming valley dribbles the Senne (whence, I suppose, is derived Senna), the most nauseous little river in the world — which receives all the outpourings of all the drains and houses and is then converted into beer for the inhabitants, all the many breweries being directly upon its edge. If you go up the hill instead of down you come to an arrangement of squares, palaces, and gardens as trim and fashionable as you will find in Europe. Thus you see that our Cybele sits with her head crowned with very stately towers and her feet in a tub of very dirty water.

"My habits here for the present year are very regular. I came here, having, as I thought, finished my work, or rather the first Part (something like three or four volumes, 8vo), but I find so much original matter here, and so many emendations to make, that I am ready to despair. However, there is nothing for it but to penelopize, pull to pieces, and stitch away again. Whatever may be the result of my labor, nobody can say that I have not worked like a brute beast, — but I don't care for the result. The labor is in itself its own reward and all I want. I go day after day to the archives here (as I went all summer at the Hague) studying

Section X. 1853.

Letter from Brussels.

the old letters and documents of the fifteenth century. Here I remain among my fellow-worms, feeding on these musty mulberry-leaves, out of which we are afterwards to spin our silk. How can you expect anything interesting from such a human cocoon? It is, however, not without its amusement in a mouldy sort of way, this reading of dead letters. It is something to read the real, bona fide signs-manual of such fellows as William of Orange, Count Egmont, Alexander Farnese, Philip II., Cardinal Granvelle, and the rest of them. It gives a 'realizing sense,' as the Americans have it. . . . . There are not many public resources of amusement in this place, — if we wanted them, — which we don't. I miss the Dresden Gallery very much, and it makes me sad to think that I shall never look at the face of the Sistine Madonna again, — that picture beyond all pictures in the world — in which the artist certainly did get to heaven and painted a face which was never seen on earth — so pathetic, so gentle, so passionless, so prophetic. . . . . There are a few good Rubenses here, — but the great wealth of that master is in Antwerp. The great picture of the Descent from the Cross is free again after having been ten years in the repairing room. It has come out in very good condition. What a picture! It seems to me as if I had really stood at the cross and seen Mary weep-

Section X. 1853.

Letter from Brussels.

ing on John's shoulder, and Magdalen receiving the dead body of the Saviour in her arms. Never was the grand tragedy represented in so profound and dramatic a manner. For it is not only in his *color* in which this man so easily surpasses all the world, but in his life-like, flesh-and-blood action, — the tragic power of his composition. And is it not appalling to think of the "large constitution of this man," when you reflect on the acres of canvas which he has covered? How inspiriting to see with what muscular, masculine vigor this splendid Fleming rushed in and plucked up drowning Art by the locks when it was sinking in the trashy sea of such creatures as the Luca Giordanos and Pietro Cortonas and the like. Well might Guido exclaim, 'The fellow mixes blood with his colors!' .... How providentially did the man come in and invoke living, breathing, moving men and women out of his canvas! Sometimes he is ranting and exaggerated, as are all men of great genius who wrestle with Nature so boldly. No doubt his heroines are more expansively endowed than would be thought genteel in our country, where cryptogams are so much in fashion, nevertheless there is always something very tremendous about him, and very often much that is sublime, pathetic, and moving. I defy any one of the average amount of imagination and sentiment to stand long before the Descent from the

Letter from Brussels.

Cross without being moved more nearly to tears than he would care to acknowledge. As for color, his effects are as sure as those of the sun rising in a tropical landscape. There is something quite genial in the cheerful sense of his own omnipotence which always inspired him. There are a few fine pictures of his here, and I go in sometimes of a raw, foggy morning merely to warm myself in the blaze of their beauty."

I have been more willing to give room to this description of Rubens's pictures and the effect they produced upon Motley, because there is a certain affinity between those sumptuous and glowing works of art and the prose pictures of the historian who so admired them. He was himself a colorist in language, and called up the image of a great personage or a splendid pageant of the past with the same affluence, the same rich vitality, that floods and warms the vast areas of canvas over which the full-fed genius of Rubens disported itself in the luxury of imaginative creation.

XI.

Publication of his first Historical Work, "Rise of the Dutch Republic." — Its Reception. — Critical Notices. — His Visit to America. (*1856–1857.*)

SECTION XI. 1856.

His manuscript finished.

THE labor of ten years was at last finished. Carrying his formidable manuscript with him, — and how formidable the manuscript which melts down into three solid octavo volumes is, only writers and publishers know, — he knocked at the gate of that terrible fortress from which Lintot and Curll and Tonson looked down on the authors of an older generation. So large a work as the History of the Rise of the Dutch Republic, offered for the press by an author as yet unknown to the British public, could hardly expect a warm welcome from the great dealers in literature as merchandise. Mr. Murray civilly declined the manuscript which was offered to him, and it was published at its author's expense by Mr. John Chapman. The time came when the positions of the first-named celebrated publisher and the unknown writer were reversed. Mr. Murray wrote to Mr. Motley asking to be allowed to publish his second great work, the History of the United

Seeks a publisher.

Publishes at his own expense.

Mr. Murray.

Netherlands, expressing at the same time his regret at what he candidly called his mistake in the first instance, and thus they were at length brought into business connection as well as the most agreeable and friendly relations. An American edition was published by the Harpers at the same time as the London one.

"Rise of the Dutch Republic" published in England and America.

If the new work of the unknown author found it difficult to obtain a publisher, it was no sooner given to the public than it found an approving, an admiring, an enthusiastic world of readers, and a noble welcome at the colder hands of the critics.

Its reception.

The Westminster Review for April, 1856, had for its leading article a paper by Mr. Froude, in which the critic awarded the highest praise to the work of the new historian. As one of the earliest as well as one of the most important recognitions of the work, I quote some of its judgments.

Mr. Froude's critical article.

"A history as complete as industry and genius can make it now lies before us of the first twenty years of the Revolt of the United Provinces; of the period in which those provinces finally conquered their independence and established the Republic of Holland. It has been the result of many years of silent, thoughtful, unobtrusive labor, and unless we are strangely mistaken, unless we are ourselves altogether unfit for this office of criticising which we have here undertaken, the book is one

SECTION XI. 1856.

Mr. Froude warmly praises it.

which will take its place among the finest histories in this or in any language. . . . . All the essentials of a great writer Mr. Motley eminently possesses. His mind is broad, his industry unwearied. In power of dramatic description no modern historian, except perhaps Mr. Carlyle, surpasses him, and in analysis of character he is elaborate and distinct. His principles are those of honest love for all which is good and admirable in human character wherever he finds it, while he unaffectedly hates oppression, and despises selfishness with all his heart."

After giving a slight analytical sketch of the series of events related in the history, Mr. Froude objects to only one of the historian's estimates, that, namely, of the course of Queen Elizabeth. "It is ungracious, however," he says, "even to find so slight a fault with these admirable volumes. Mr. Motley has written without haste, with the leisurely composure of a master. . . . . We now take our leave of Mr. Motley, desiring him only to accept our hearty thanks for these volumes, which we trust will soon take their place in every English library. Our quotations will have sufficed to show the ability of the writer. Of the scope and general character of his work we have given but a languid conception. The true merit of a great book must be learned from the book itself. Our part has been rather to select varied specimens of style and power.

Of Mr. Motley's antecedents we know nothing. If he has previously appeared before the public, his reputation has not crossed the Atlantic. It will not be so now. We believe that we may promise him as warm a welcome among ourselves as he will receive even in America; that his place will be at once conceded to him among the first historians in our common language."

"Rise of the Dutch Republic."

The faithful and unwearied Mr. Allibone has swept the whole field of contemporary criticism, and shown how wide and universal was the welcome accorded to the hitherto unknown author. An article headed "Prescott and Motley," attributed to M. Guizot, which must have been translated, I suppose, from his own language, judging by its freedom from French idioms, is to be found in the Edinburgh Review for January, 1857. The praise, not unmingled with criticisms, which that great historian bestowed upon Motley is less significant than the fact that he superintended a translation of the Rise of the Dutch Republic, and himself wrote the Introduction to it.

Mr. Allibone's citations.

M. Guizot superintends a translation.

A general chorus of approbation followed or accompanied these leading voices. The reception of the work in Great Britain was a triumph. On the Continent, in addition to the tribute paid to it by M. Guizot, it was translated into Dutch, into Ger-

Translations.

Section XI. 1856.

"Rise of the Dutch Republic."

The North American Review.

man, and into Russian. At home his reception was not less hearty. The North American Review, which had set its foot on the semi-autobiographical medley which he called "Morton's Hope," which had granted a decent space and a tepid recognition to his "semi-historical" romance, in which he had already given the reading public a taste of his quality as a narrator of real events and a delineator of real personages, — this old and awe-inspiring New England and more than New England representative of the Fates, found room for a long and most laudatory article, in which the son of one of our most distinguished historians did the honors of the venerable literary periodical to the new-comer, for whom the folding-doors of all the critical head-quarters were flying open as if of themselves. Mr. Allibone has recorded the opinions of some of our best scholars as expressed to him.

Dr. Lieber.

Dr. Lieber wrote a letter to Mr. Allibone in the strongest terms of praise. I quote one passage which in the light of after events borrows a cruel significance.

"Congress and Parliament decree thanks for military exploits, — rarely for diplomatic achievements. If they ever voted their thanks for books, — and what deeds have influenced the course of human events more than some books? — Motley ought to have the thanks of our Congress; but I doubt not that he has already the thanks of every American who has read the work. It will leave its distinct mark upon the American mind."

" Rise of the Dutch Republic."

Mr. Everett writes: —

Mr. Everett.

"Mr. Motley's History of the Dutch Republic is in my judgment a work of the highest merit. Unwearying research for years in the libraries of Europe, patience and judgment in arranging and digesting his materials, a fine historical tact, much skill in characterization, the perspective of narration, as it may be called, and a vigorous style unite to make it a very capital work, and place the name of Motley by the side of those of our great historical trio, — Bancroft, Irving, and Prescott."

Mr. Irving, Mr. Bancroft, Mr. Sumner, Mr. Hillard, united their voices in the same strain of commendation. Mr. Prescott, whose estimate of the new History is of peculiar value for obvious reasons, writes to Mr. Allibone thus: —

Mr. Prescott.

"The opinion of any individual seems superfluous in respect to a work on the merits of which the public both at home and abroad have pronounced so unanimous a verdict. As Motley's path crosses my own historic field, I may be thought to possess some advantage over most critics in my familiarity with the ground.

"However this may be, I can honestly bear my testimony to the extent of his researches and to

Section XI. 1856.

"Rise of the Dutch Republic."

Mr. Prescott.

the accuracy with which he has given the results of them to the public. Far from making his book a mere register of events, he has penetrated deep below the surface and explored the cause of these events. He has carefully studied the physiognomy of the times and given finished portraits of the great men who conducted the march of the revolution. Every page is instinct with the love of freedom and with that personal knowledge of the working of free institutions which could alone enable him to do justice to his subject. We may congratulate ourselves that it was reserved for one of our countrymen to tell the story — better than it had yet been told — of this memorable revolution, which in so many of its features bears a striking resemblance to our own."

Reception of the work by the public.

The public welcomed the work as cordially as the critics. Fifteen thousand copies had already been sold in London in 1857. In America it was equally popular. Its author saw his name enrolled by common consent among those of the great writers of his time. Europe accepted him, his country was proud to claim him, scholarship set its jealously guarded seal upon the result of his labors, the reading world, which had not cared greatly for his stories, hung in delight over a narrative more exciting than romances; and the lonely student, who had almost forgotten the look of living men in the solitude of archives haunted by dead memories, found himself suddenly in the full blaze of a great reputation.

XII.

Visit to America. — Residence in Boylston Place.
(1856 - 1857.)

SECT. XII. 1856 - 1857.

Comes to America.

A winter in Boston.

HE visited this country in 1856, and spent the winter of 1856 - 57 in Boston, living with his family in a house in Boylston Place. At this time I had the pleasure of meeting him often, and of seeing the changes which maturity, success, the opening of a great literary and social career, had wrought in his character and bearing. He was in every way greatly improved; the interesting, impulsive youth had ripened into a noble manhood. Dealing with great themes, his own mind had gained their dignity. Accustomed to the company of dead statesmen and heroes, his own ideas had risen to a higher standard. The flattery of society had added a new grace to his natural modesty. He was now a citizen of the world by his reputation; the past was his province, in which he was recognized as a master; the idol's pedestal was ready for him, but he betrayed no desire to show himself upon it.

XIII.

Return to England. — Social Relations. — Lady Harcourt's Letter. (1858-1860.)

SECT. XIII. 1858.

DURING the years spent in Europe in writing his first History, from 1851 to 1856, Mr. Motley had lived a life of great retirement and simplicity, devoting himself to his work and to the education of his children, to which last object he was always ready to give the most careful supervision. He was as yet unknown beyond the circle of his friends, and he did not seek society. In this quiet way he had passed the two years of residence in Dresden, the year divided between Brussels and the Hague, and a very tranquil year spent at Vevay on the Lake of Geneva. His health at this time was tolerably good, except for nervous headaches, which frequently recurred and were of great severity. His visit to England with his manuscript in search of a publisher has already been mentioned.

Revisits England.

In 1858 he revisited England. His fame as a successful author was there before him, and he naturally became the object of many attentions. He now made many acquaintances who afterwards be-

SECT. XIII. 1858.

Social life.

came his kind and valued friends. Among those mentioned by his daughter, Lady Harcourt, are Lord Lyndhurst, Lord Carlisle, Lady William Russell, Lord and Lady Palmerston, Dean Milman, with many others. The following winter was passed in Rome, among many English and American friends.

Lady Harcourt's etter.

"In the course of the next summer," his daughter writes to me, "we all went to England, and for the next two years, marked chiefly by the success of the 'United Netherlands,' our social life was most agreeable and most interesting. He was in the fulness of his health and powers; his works had made him known in intellectual society, and I think his presence, on the other hand, increased their effects. As no one knows better than you do, his belief in his own country and in its institutions at their best was so passionate and intense that it was a part of his nature, yet his refined and fastidious tastes were deeply gratified by the influences of his life in England, and the spontaneous kindness which he received added much to his happiness. At that time Lord Palmerston was Prime Minister; the weekly receptions at Cambridge House were the centre of all that was brilliant in the political and social world, while Lansdowne House, Holland House, and others were open to the *sommités* in all

Social life.

branches of literature, science, rank, and politics. .... It was the last year of Lord Macaulay's life, and as a few out of many names which I recall come Dean Milman, Mr. Froude (whose review of the Dutch Republic in the Westminster was one of the first warm recognitions it ever received), the Duke and Duchess of Argyll, Sir William Stirling Maxwell, then Mr. Stirling of Keir, the Sheridan family in its different brilliant members, Lord Wensleydale, and many more."

There was no society to which Motley would not have added grace and attraction by his presence, and to say that he was a welcome guest in the best houses of England is only saying that these houses are always open to those whose abilities, characters, achievements, are commended to the circles that have the best choice by the personal gifts which are nature's passport everywhere.

XIV.

Letter to Mr. Francis H. Underwood. — Plan of Mr. Motley's Historical Works. — Second Great Work, "History of the United Netherlands." (*1859.*)

Sect. XIV. 1859.

Letter to Mr. Underwood.

I am enabled by the kindness of Mr. Francis H. Underwood to avail myself of a letter addressed to him by Mr. Motley in the year before the publication of this second work, which gives us an insight into his mode of working and the plan he proposed to follow. It begins with an allusion which recalls a literary event interesting to many of his American friends.

Rome, March 4, 1859.

F. H. Underwood, Esq.

The Atlantic Monthly.

My dear Sir, — . . . . I am delighted to hear of the great success of the Atlantic Monthly. In this remote region I have not the chance of reading it as often as I should like, but from the specimens which I have seen I am quite sure it deserves its wide circulation. A serial publication, the contents of which are purely original and of such remarkable merit, is a novelty in our country, and I am de-

Letter to Mr. Underwood.

lighted to find that it has already taken so prominent a position before the reading world. . . . .

The whole work [his history], of which the three volumes already published form a part, will be called "The Eighty Years' War for Liberty."

Plans for a great history.

Epoch I. is the Rise of the Dutch Republic.

Epoch II. Independence Achieved. From the Death of William the Silent till the Twelve Years' Truce. 1584 – 1609.

Epoch III. Independence Recognized. From the Twelve Years' Truce to the Peace of Westphalia. 1609 – 1648.

My subject is a very vast one, for the struggle of the United Provinces with Spain was one in which all the leading states of Europe were more or less involved. After the death of William the Silent, the history assumes world-wide proportions. Thus the volume which I am just about terminating.... is almost as much English history as Dutch. The Earl of Leicester, very soon after the death of Orange, was appointed governor of the provinces, and the alliance between the two countries almost amounted to a political union. I shall try to get the whole of the Leicester administration, terminating with the grand drama of the Invincible Armada, into one volume; but I doubt, my materials are so enormous. I have been personally very hard at

SECT. XIV. 1859.

Letter to Mr. Underwood.

work, nearly two years, ransacking the British State Paper Office, the British Museum, and the Holland archives, and I have had two copyists constantly engaged in London, and two others at the Hague. Besides this, I passed the whole of last winter at Brussels, where, by special favor of the Belgian Government, I was allowed to read what no one else has ever been permitted to see, — the great mass of copies taken by that Government from the Simancas archives, a translated epitome of which has been published by Gachard. This correspondence reaches to the death of Philip II., and is of immense extent and importance. Had I not obtained leave to read the invaluable and, for my purpose, indispensable documents at Brussels, I should have gone to Spain, for they will not be published these twenty years, and then only in a translated and excessively abbreviated and unsatisfactory form. I have read the whole of this correspondence, and made very copious notes of it. In truth, I devoted three months of last winter to that purpose alone.

Plans and labors.

The materials I have collected from the English archives are also extremely important and curious. I have hundreds of interesting letters never published or to be published, by Queen Elizabeth, Burghley, Walsingham, Sidney, Drake, Willoughby, Leicester, and others. For the whole of that portion of my subject in which Holland and England were combined into one whole, to resist Spain in its attempt to obtain the universal empire, I have very abundant collections. For the history of the United Provinces is not at all a provincial history. It is the history of European liberty. Without the struggle of Holland and England against Spain, all Europe might have been Catholic and Spanish. It was Holland that saved England in the sixteenth century, and, by so doing, secured the triumph of the Reformation, and placed the independence of the various states of Europe upon a sure foundation. Of course, the materials collected by me at the Hague are of great importance. As a single specimen, I will state that I found in the archives there an immense and confused mass of papers, which turned out to be the autograph letters of Olden Barneveld during the last few years of his life; during, in short, the whole of that most important period which preceded his execution. These letters are in such an intolerable handwriting that no one has ever attempted to read them. I could read them only imperfectly myself, and it would have taken me a very long time to have acquired the power to do so; but my copyist and reader there is the most patient and indefatigable person alive, and he has quite mastered the handwriting, and he writes me that they are a mine of historical wealth

Letter to Mr. Underwood.

Materials for his history.

Sect. XIV. 1859.

Letter to Mr. Underwood.

for me. I shall have complete copies before I get to that period, one of signal interest, and which has never been described. I mention these matters that you may see that my work, whatever its other value may be, is built upon the only foundation fit for history, — original contemporary documents. These are all unpublished. Of course, I use the contemporary historians and pamphleteers, — Dutch, Spanish, French, Italian, German, and English, — but the most valuable of my sources are manuscript ones. I have said the little which I have said in order to vindicate the largeness of the subject. The kingdom of Holland is a small power now, but the Eighty Years' War, which secured the civil and religious independence of the Dutch Commonwealth and of Europe, was the great event of that whole age.

Plan of his whole work.

The whole work will therefore cover a most remarkable epoch in human history, from the abdication of Charles Fifth to the Peace of Westphalia, at which last point the political and geographical arrangements of Europe were established on a permanent basis, — in the main undisturbed until the French Revolution. . . . .

I will mention that I received yesterday a letter from the distinguished M. Guizot, informing me that the first volume of the French translation, edited by him, with an introduction, has just been

Sect. XIV. 1859.

Letter to Mr. Under-Wood.

published. The publication was hastened in consequence of the appearance of a rival translation at Brussels. The German translation is very elegantly and expensively printed in handsome octavos; and the Dutch translation, under the editorship of the archivist general of Holland, Bakhuyzen v. d. Brink, is enriched with copious notes and comments by that distinguished scholar.

Translations and reprints.

There are also three different piratical reprints of the original work at Amsterdam, Leipzig, and London. I must add that I had nothing to do with the translation in any case. In fact, with the exception of M. Guizot, no one ever obtained permission of me to publish translations, and I never knew of the existence of them until I read of it in the journals. . . . . I forgot to say that among the collections already thoroughly examined by me is that portion of the Simancas archives still retained in the Imperial archives of France. I spent a considerable time in Paris for the purpose of reading these documents. There are many letters of Philip II. there, with *apostilles* by his own hand. . . . . I would add that I am going to pass this summer at Venice for the purpose of reading and procuring copies from the very rich archives of that Republic, of the correspondence of their envoys in Madrid, London, and Brussels during the epoch of which I am treating. I am also not without hope

Sect. XIV. 1859.

of gaining access to the archives of the Vatican here, although there are some difficulties in the way.

With kind regards . . . .

I remain very truly yours,

J. L. MOTLEY.

XV.

Publication of the first two Volumes of the "History of the United Netherlands."— Their Reception. (1860.)

SECTION XV. 1860.

WE know something of the manner in which Mr. Motley collected his materials. We know the labors, the difficulties, the cost of his toils among the dusty records of the past. What he gained by the years he spent in his researches is so well stated by himself that I shall borrow his own words: —

Study in State archives.

"Thanks to the liberality of many modern governments of Europe, the archives where the state secrets of the buried centuries have so long mouldered are now open to the student of history. To him who has patience and industry, many mysteries are thus revealed which no political sagacity or critical acumen could have divined. He leans over the shoulder of Philip the Second at his writing-table, as the King spells patiently out, with cipher-key in hand, the most concealed hieroglyphics of Parma, or Guise, or Mendoza. He reads the secret thoughts of 'Fabius' [Philip II.] as that cunctative Roman scrawls his marginal apostilles

SECTION XV. 1860.

on each despatch; he pries into all the stratagems of Camillus, Hortensius, Mucius, Julius, Tullius, and the rest of those ancient heroes who lent their names to the diplomatic masqueraders of the sixteenth century; he enters the cabinet of the deeply pondering Burghley, and takes from the most private drawer the memoranda which record that minister's unutterable doubtings; he pulls from the dressing-gown folds of the stealthy, soft-gliding Walsingham the last secret which he has picked from the Emperor's pigeon-holes or the Pope's pocket, and which not Hatton, nor Buckhurst, nor Leicester, nor the Lord Treasurer is to see; nobody but Elizabeth herself; he sits invisible at the most secret councils of the Nassaus and Barneveldt and Buys, or pores with Farnese over coming victories and vast schemes of universal conquest; he reads the latest bit of scandal, the minutest characteristic of king or minister, chronicled by the gossiping Venetians for the edification of the Forty; and after all this prying and eavesdropping, having seen the cross-purposes, the bribings, the windings in the dark, he is not surprised if those who were systematically deceived did not always arrive at correct conclusions." (*Hist. of United Netherlands,* I. p. 54.)

Revelation of state secrets.

The fascination of such a quest is readily conceivable. A drama with real characters, and the spectator at liberty to go behind the scenes and look upon and talk with the kings and queens between the acts; to examine the scenery, to handle the properties, to study the "make up" of the imposing personages of full-dress histories; to deal with them all as Thackeray has done with the Grand Monarque in one of his caustic sketches, — this would be as exciting, one might suppose, as to sit through a play one knows by heart at Drury Lane or the Théâtre Français, and might furnish occupation enough to the curious idler who was only in search of entertainment. The mechanical obstacles of half-illegible manuscript, of antiquated forms of speech, to say nothing of the intentional obscurities of diplomatic correspondence, stand, however, in the way of all but the resolute and unwearied scholar. These difficulties, in all their complex obstinacy, had been met and overcome by the heroic efforts, the concentrated devotion, of the new laborer in the unbroken fields of secret history.

Without stopping to take breath, as it were, — for his was a task *de longue haleine*, — he proceeded to his second great undertaking.

Second historical work, History of the United Netherlands.

The first portion — consisting of two volumes — of the History of the United Netherlands was published in the year 1860. It maintained and increased the reputation he had already gained by his first history.

SECTION XV. 1860.

The London Quarterly Review devoted a long article to it, beginning with this handsome tribute to his earlier and later volumes: —

History of the United Netherlands.

The Quarterly Review.

"Mr. Motley's 'History of the Rise of the Dutch Republic' is already known and valued for the grasp of mind which it displays, for the earnest and manly spirit in which he has communicated the results of deep research and careful reflection. Again he appears before us, rich with the spoils of time, to tell the story of the United Netherlands from the time of William the Silent to the end of the eventful year of the Spanish Armada, and we still find him in every way worthy of this 'great argument.' Indeed, it seems to us that he proceeds with an increased facility of style, and with a more complete and easy command over his materials. These materials are indeed splendid, and of them most excellent use has been made. The English State Paper Office, the Spanish archives from Simancas, and the Dutch and Belgian repositories, have all yielded up their secrets; and Mr. Motley has enjoyed the advantage of dealing with a vast mass of unpublished documents, of which he has not failed to avail himself to an extent which places his work in the foremost rank as an authority for the period to which it relates. By means of his labor and his art we can sit at the council

History of the United Netherlands.

board of Philip and Elizabeth, we can read their most private despatches. Guided by his demonstration, we are enabled to dissect out to their ultimate issues the minutest ramifications of intrigue. We join in the amusement of the popular lampoon; we visit the prison-house; we stand by the scaffold; we are present at the battle and the siege. We can scan the inmost characters of men and can view them in their habits as they lived."

After a few criticisms upon lesser points of form and style, the writer says:—

The London Quarterly Review.

"But the work itself must be read to appreciate the vast and conscientious industry bestowed upon it. His delineations are true and life-like, because they are not mere compositions written to please the ear, but are really taken from the facts and traits preserved in those authentic records to which he has devoted the labor of many years. Diligent and painstaking as the humblest chronicler, he has availed himself of many sources of information which have not been made use of by any previous historical writer. At the same time he is not oppressed by his materials, but has sagacity to estimate their real value, and he has combined with scholarly power the facts which they contain. He has rescued the story of the Netherlands from the domain of vague and general narrative, and has labored, with much judgment and ability, to unfold

SECTION XV. 1860.

History of the United Netherlands.

The Edinburgh Review.

the *Belli causas, et vitia, et modos,* and to assign to every man and every event their own share in the contest, and their own influence upon its fortunes. We do not wonder that his earlier publication has been received as a valuable addition, not only to English, but to European literature." One or two other contemporary criticisms may help us with their side lights. A critic in the Edinburgh Review for January, 1861, thinks that "Mr. Motley has not always been successful in keeping the graphic variety of his details subordinate to the main theme of his work." Still, he excuses the fault, as he accounts it, in consideration of the new light thrown on various obscure points of history, and "it is atoned for by striking merits, by many narratives of great events faithfully, powerfully, and vividly executed, by the clearest and most life-like conceptions of character, and by a style which, if it sacrifices the severer principles of composition to a desire to be striking and picturesque, is always vigorous, full of animation, and glowing with the genuine enthusiasm of the writer. Mr. Motley combines as an historian two qualifications seldom found united, — to great capacity for historical research he adds much power of pictorial representation. In his pages we find characters and scenes minutely set forth in elaborate and characteristic detail, which is relieved and

History of the United Netherlands.

heightened in effect by the artistic breadth of light and shade thrown across the broader prospects of history. In an American author, too, we must commend the hearty English spirit in which the book is written; and fertile as the present age has been in historical works of the highest merit, none of them can be ranked above these volumes in the grand qualities of interest, accuracy, and truth."

Blackwood's Magazine.

A writer in Blackwood (May, 1861) contrasts Motley with Froude somewhat in the way in which another critic had contrasted him with Prescott. Froude, he says, remembers that there are some golden threads in the black robe of the Dominican. Motley "finds it black and thrusts it farther into the darkness."

A writer's character seen in his books.

Every writer carries more or less of his own character into his book, of course. A great professor has told me that there is a personal flavor in the mathematical work of a man of genius like Poisson. Those who have known Motley and Prescott would feel sure beforehand that the impulsive nature of the one and the judicial serenity of the other would as surely betray themselves in their writings as in their conversation and in their every movement. Another point which the critic of Blackwood's Magazine has noticed has not been

SECTION XV. 1860.

History of the United Netherlands.

so generally observed: it is what he calls "a dashing, offhand, rattling" style, — "*fast*" writing. It cannot be denied that here and there may be detected slight vestiges of the way of writing of an earlier period of Motley's literary life, with which I have no reason to think the writer just mentioned was acquainted. Now and then I can trace in the turn of a phrase, in the twinkle of an epithet, a faint reminiscence of a certain satirical levity, airiness, jauntiness, if I may hint such a word, which is just enough to remind me of those perilous shallows of his early time through which his richly freighted argosy had passed with such wonderful escape from their dangers and such very slight marks of injury. That which is pleasant gayety in conversation may be quite out of place in formal composition, and Motley's wit must have had a hard time of it struggling to show its spangles in the processions while his gorgeous tragedies went sweeping by.

Traces of his earlier style.

XVI.

Residence in England — Outbreak of the Civil War. — Letter to the London Times. — Visit to America. — Appointed Minister to Austria. — Lady Harcourt's Letter. — Miss Motley's Memorandum. (1860-1866.)

SECT. XVI. 1860.

THE winter of 1859-60 was passed chiefly at Oatlands Hotel, Walton-on-Thames. In 1860 Mr. Motley hired the house No. 31 Hertford Street, May Fair, London. He had just published the first two volumes of his History of the Netherlands, and was ready for the further labors of its continuation, when the threats, followed by the outbreak, of the great civil contention in his native land brought him back from the struggles of the sixteenth and seventeenth centuries to the conflict of the nineteenth.

The civil war in America.

His love of country, which had grown upon him so remarkably of late years, would not suffer him to be silent at such a moment. All around him he found ignorance and prejudice. The quarrel was like to be prejudged in default of a champion of

SECT. XVI. 1861.

Letters to The London Times.

the cause which to him was that of Liberty and Justice. He wrote two long letters to the London Times, in which he attempted to make clear to Englishmen and to Europe the nature and conditions of our complex system of government, the real cause of the strife, and the mighty issues at stake. Nothing could have been more timely, nothing nore needed. Mr. William Everett, who was then in England, bears strong testimony to the effect these letters produced. Had Mr. Motley done no other service to his country, this alone would entitle him to honorable remembrance as among the first defenders of the flag which at that moment had more to fear from what was going on in the cabinet councils of Europe than from all the armed hosts that were gathering against it.

Return to America.

He returned to America in 1861 and soon afterwards was appointed by Mr. Lincoln Minister to Austria. Mr. Burlingame had been previously appointed to the office, but having been objected to by the Austrian Government for political reasons, the place unexpectedly left vacant was conferred upon Motley, who had no expectation of any diplomatic appointment when he left Europe. For some interesting particulars relating to his residence in Vienna I must refer to the communications addressed to me by his daughter, Lady Harcourt, and her youngest sister, and the letters

Appointed Minister to Austria.

I received from him while at the Austrian capital. Lady Harcourt writes : —

SECT. XVI. 1860–1866.

Lady Harcourt's letter.

"He held the post for six years, seeing the civil war fought out and brought to a triumphant conclusion, and enjoying, as I have every reason to believe, the full confidence and esteem of Mr. Lincoln to the last hour of the President's life. In the first dark years the painful interest of the great national drama was so all-absorbing that literary work was entirely put aside, and with his countrymen at home he lived only in the varying fortunes of the day, his profound faith and enthusiasm sustaining him and lifting him above the natural influence of a by no means sanguine temperament. Later, when the tide was turning and success was nearing, he was more able to work. His social relations during the whole period of his mission were of the most agreeable character. The society of Vienna was at that time, and I believe is still, the absolute reverse of that of England, where all claims to distinction are recognized and welcomed. There the old feudal traditions were still in full force, and diplomatic representatives admitted to the court society by right of official position found it to consist exclusively of an aristocracy of birth, sixteen quarterings of nobility being necessary to a right of presentation to the Emperor and Empress. The society thus constituted was distinguished by

Society of Vienna.

Society of Vienna.

great charm and grace of manner, the exclusion of all outer elements not only limiting the numbers, but giving the ease of a family party within the charmed circle. On the other hand, larger interests suffered under the rigid exclusion of all occupations except the army, diplomacy, and court place. The intimacy among the different members of the society was so close that, beyond a courtesy of manner that never failed, the tendency was to resist the approach of any stranger as a *gêne*. A single new face was instantly remarked and commented on in a Vienna saloon to an extent unknown in any other large capital. This peculiarity, however, worked in favor of the old resident. Kindliness of feeling increased with familiarity and grew into something better than acquaintance, and the parting with most sincere and affectionately disposed friends in the end was deeply felt on both sides. Those years were passed in a pleasant house in the Weiden Faubourg, with a large garden at the back, and I do not think that during this time there was one disagreeable incident in his relations to his colleagues, while in several cases the relations, agreeable with all, became those of close friendship. We lived constantly, of course, in diplomatic and Austrian society, and during the latter part of the time particularly his house was as much frequented and the centre of as many dancing and other recep-

Residence at Vienna.

tions as any in the place. His official relations with the Foreign Office were courteous and agreeable, the successive Foreign Ministers during his stay being Count Richberg, Count Mensdorff, and Baron Beust. Austria was so far removed from any real contact with our own country that, though the interest in our war may have been languid, they did not pretend to a knowledge which might have inclined them to controversy, while an instinct that we were acting as a constituted government against rebellion rather inclined them to sympathy. I think I may say that as he became known among them his keen patriotism and high sense of honor and truth were fully understood and appreciated, and that what he said always commanded a sympathetic hearing among men with totally different political ideas, but with chivalrous and loyal instincts to comprehend his own. I shall never forget his account of the terrible day when the news of Mr. Lincoln's death came. By some accident a rumor of it reached him first through a colleague. He went straight to the Foreign Office for news, hoping against hope, was received by Count Mensdorff, who merely came forward and laid his arm about his shoulder with an intense sympathy beyond words."

Official relations.

Miss Motley, the historian's youngest daughter has added a note to her sister's communication:

SECT. XVI. 1860-1866.

Miss Motley's note.

"During his residence in Vienna the most important negotiations which he had to carry on with the Austrian Government were those connected with the Mexican affair. Maximilian at one time applied to his brother the Emperor for assistance, and he promised to accede to his demand. Accordingly a large number of volunteers were equipped and had actually embarked at Trieste, when a despatch from Seward arrived, instructing the American Minister to give notice to the Austrian Government that if the troops sailed for Mexico he was to leave Vienna at once. My father had to go at once to Count Mensdorff with these instructions, and in spite of the Foreign Minister being annoyed that the United States Government had not sooner intimated that this extreme course would be taken, the interview was quite amicable and the troops were not allowed to sail. We were in Vienna during the war in which Denmark fought alone against Austria and Prussia, and when it was over Bismarck came to Vienna to settle the terms of peace with the Emperor. He dined with us twice during his short stay and was most delightful and agreeable. When he and my father were together they seemed to live over the youthful days they had spent together as students, and many were the anecdotes of their boyish frolics which Bismarck related."

Troops for Mexico detained.

Visits from Bismarck.

XVII.

Letters from Vienna. (1861-1863.)

Sect. XVII. 1861-1863.

Soon after Mr. Motley's arrival in Vienna I received a long letter from him, most of which relates to personal matters, but which contains a few sentences of interest to the general reader as showing his zealous labors, wherever he found himself, in behalf of the great cause then in bloody debate in his own country: —

"November 14, 1861.

Letter from Vienna.

". . . . What can I say to you of cis-Atlantic things? I am almost ashamed to be away from home. You know that I had decided to remain, and had sent for my family to come to America, when my present appointment altered my plans. I do what good I can. I think I made some impression on Lord John Russell, with whom I spent two days soon after my arrival in England, and I talked very frankly and as strongly as I could to Palmerston, and I have had long conversations and correspondences with other leading men in England. I have also had an hour's [conversation] with Thouvenel

SECT. XVII. 1861.

Letter from Vienna.

in Paris. I hammered the Northern view into him as soundly as I could. For this year there will be no foreign interference with us. I don't anticipate it at any time, unless we bring it on ourselves by bad management, which I don't expect. Our fate is in our own hands, and Europe is looking on to see which side is strongest,— when it has made the discovery it will back it as also the best and the most moral. Yesterday I had my audience with the Emperor. He received me with much cordiality, and seemed interested in a long account which I gave him of our affairs. You may suppose I inculcated the Northern views. We spoke in his vernacular, and he asked me afterwards if I was a German. I mention this not from vanity, but because he asked it with earnestness, and as if it had a political significance. Of course I undeceived him. His appearance interested me, and his manner is very pleasing."

I continued to receive long and interesting letters from him at intervals during his residence as Minister at Vienna. Relating as they often did to public matters, about which he had private sources of information, his anxiety that they should not get into print was perfectly natural. As, however, I was at liberty to read his letters to others at my discretion, and as many parts of these letters have an interest as showing how American affairs looked to one who was behind the scenes in Europe, I may venture to give some extracts without fear of violating the spirit of his injunctions, or of giving offence to individuals. The time may come when his extended correspondence can be printed in full with propriety, but it must be in a future year and after it has passed into the hands of a younger generation. Meanwhile, these few glimpses at his life and records of his feelings and opinions will help to make the portrait of the man we are studying present itself somewhat more clearly.

"Legation of the U. S. A., Vienna, January 14, 1862.

Letter from Vienna.

"My dear Holmes, — I have two letters of yours, November 29 and December 17, to express my thanks for. It is quite true that it is difficult for me to write with the same feeling that inspires you, — that everything around the inkstand within a radius of a thousand miles is full of deepest interest to writer and reader. I don't even intend to try to amuse you with Vienna matters. What is it to you that we had a very pleasant dinner-party last week at Prince Esterhazy's, and another this week at Prince Liechtenstein's, and that to-morrow I am to put on my cocked hat and laced coat to make a visit to her Imperial Majesty, the Empress Mother,

SECT. XVII. 1862.

and that to-night there is to be the first of the assembly balls, the Vienna Almack's, at which — I shall be allowed to absent myself altogether?

The Trent affair.

"It strikes me that there is likely to be left a fair field for us a few months longer, say till midsummer. The Trent affair I shall not say much about, except to state that I have always been for giving up the prisoners. I was awfully afraid, knowing that the demand had gone forth, —

> 'Send us your prisoners or you'll hear of it,'

that the answer would have come back in the Hotspur vein —

> 'And if the Devil come and roar for them,
> We will not send them.'

The result would have been most disastrous, for in order to secure a most trifling advantage, — that of keeping Mason and Slidell at Fort Warren a little longer, — we should have turned our backs on all the principles maintained by us when neutral, and should have been obliged to accept a war at an enormous disadvantage. . . . .

"But I hardly dared to hope that we should have obtained such a victory as we have done. To have disavowed the illegal transaction at once, — before any demand came from England, — to have placed that disavowal on the broad ground of principle which we have always cherished, and thus with a clear conscience, and to our entire honor, to have kept ourselves clear from a war which must have given the Confederacy the invincible alliance of England,—was exactly what our enemies in Europe did not suppose us capable of doing. But we have done it in the handsomest manner, and there is not one liberal heart in this hemisphere that is not rejoiced, nor one hater of us and of our institutions that is not gnashing his teeth with rage."

The letter of ten close pages from which I have quoted these passages is full of confidential information, and contains extracts from letters of leading statesmen. If its date had been 1762, I might feel authorized in disobeying its injunctions of privacy. I must quote one other sentence, as it shows his animus at that time towards a distinguished statesman of whom he was afterwards accused of speaking in very hard terms by an obscure writer whose intent was to harm him. In speaking of the Trent affair, Mr. Motley says: "The English premier has been foiled by our much maligned Secretary of State, of whom, on this occasion at least, one has the right to say, with Sir Henry Wotton,—

Mr. Seward.

His armor was his honest thought
And simple truth his utmost skill."

SECT. XVII. 1862.

He thinks of nothing but American affairs.

He says at the close of this long letter: "I wish I could bore you about something else but American politics. But there is nothing else *worth* thinking of in the world. All else is leather and prunella. We are living over again the days of the Dutchmen or the seventeenth-century Englishmen."

My next letter, of fourteen closely written pages, was of similar character to the last. Motley could think of nothing but the great conflict. He was alive to every report from America, listening too with passionate fears or hopes, as the case might be, to the whispers not yet audible to the world which passed from lip to lip of the statesmen who were watching the course of events from the other side of the Atlantic with the sweet complacency of the looker-on of Lucretius; too often rejoicing in the storm that threatened wreck to institutions and an organization which they felt to be a standing menace to the established order of things in their older communities.

A few extracts from this very long letter will be found to have a special interest from the time at which they were written.

"LEGATION OF U. S. A., VIENNA, February 26, 1862.

Letter from Vienna.

"MY DEAR HOLMES, — . . . . I take great pleasure in reading your prophecies, and intend to be just as free in hazarding my own, for, as you say, our mor-

Letter from Vienna.

tal life is but a string of guesses at the future, and no one but an idiot would be discouraged at finding himself sometimes far out in his calculations. If I find you *signally right* in any of your predictions, be sure that I will congratulate and applaud. If you make mistakes, you shall never hear of them again, and I promise to forget them. Let me ask the same indulgence from you in return. This is what makes letter-writing a comfort and journalizing dangerous. . . . . The ides of March will be upon us before this letter reaches you. We have got to squash the rebellion soon or be squashed forever as a nation. I don't pretend to judge military plans or the capacities of generals. But, as you suggest, perhaps I can take a more just view of the whole picture of the eventful struggle at this great distance than do those absolutely acting and suffering on the scene. Nor can I resist the desire to prophesy any more than you can do, knowing that I may prove utterly mistaken. I say, then, that one great danger comes from the chance of foreign interference. What will prevent that?

The rebellion.

His prophecies.

"Our utterly defeating the Confederates in some *great* and *conclusive* battle; or,

"Our possession of the cotton-ports and opening them to European trade; or,

"A *most unequivocal policy* of slave emancipation.

"Any one of these three conditions would stave off

SECT. XVII. 1862.

Letter from Vienna.

recognition by foreign powers, until we had ourselves abandoned the attempt to reduce the South to obedience.

Slave emancipation the most important measure.

"The last measure is to my mind the most important. The South has, by going to war with the United States Government, *thrust into our hands against our will* the invincible weapon which constitutional reasons had hitherto forbidden us to employ. At the same time it has given us the power to remedy a great wrong to four millions of the human race, in which we had hitherto been obliged to acquiesce. We are threatened with national annihilation, and defied to use the only means of national preservation.

"The question is distinctly proposed to us, Shall slavery die, or the great Republic? It is most astounding to me that there can be two opinions in the free States as to the answer.

"If we do fall, we deserve our fate. At the beginning of the contest, constitutional scruples might be respectable. But now we are fighting to subjugate the South; that is, Slavery. We are fighting for nothing else that I know of. We are fighting for the Union. Who wishes to destroy the Union? The slaveholder, nobody else. Are we to spend twelve hundred millions, and raise six hundred thousand soldiers, in order to *protect* slavery? It really does seem to me too simple for argument. I

Letter from Vienna.

am anxiously waiting for the coming Columbus who will set this egg of ours on end by smashing in the slavery end. We shall be rolling about in every direction until that is done. I don't know that it is to be done by proclamation. Rather perhaps by facts. . . . . Well, I console myself with thinking that the people — the American people, at least — is about as wise collectively as less numerous collections of individuals, and that the people has really declared emancipation, and is only puzzling how to carry it into effect. After all, it seems to be a law of Providence, that progress should be by a spiral movement; so that when it seems most tortuous, we may perhaps be going ahead. I am firm in the faith that slavery is now wriggling itself to death. With slavery in its pristine vigor, I should think the restored Union neither possible nor desirable. Don't understand me as not taking into account all the strategical considerations against premature governmental utterances on this great subject. But are there any trustworthy friends to the Union among the slaveholders? Should we lose many Kentuckians and Virginians who are now with us, if we boldly confiscated the slaves of all rebels? — and a confiscation of property which has legs and so confiscates itself, at command, is not only a legal, but would prove a very practical measure in time of war. In brief, the time is fast

Slavery about to perish.

SECT. XVII. 1862.

Letter from Vienna.

approaching, I think, when 'Thorough' should be written on all our banners. Slavery will never accept a subordinate position. The great Republic and Slavery cannot both survive. We have been defied to mortal combat, and yet we hesitate to strike. These are my poor thoughts on this great subject. Perhaps you will think them crude. I was much struck with what you quote from Mr. Conway, that if emancipation was proclaimed on the Upper Mississippi it would be known to the negroes of Louisiana in advance of the telegraph. And if once the blacks had leave to run, how many whites would have to stay at home to guard their dissolving property?

Lowell's Yankee Idyl.

"You have had enough of my maunderings. But before I conclude them, may I ask you to give all our kindest regards to Lowell, and to express our admiration for the Yankee Idyl. I am afraid of using too extravagant language if I say all I think about it. Was there ever anything more stinging, more concentrated, more vigorous, more just? He has condensed into those few pages the essence of a hundred diplomatic papers and historical disquisitions and Fourth of July orations. I was dining a day or two since with his friend Lytton (Bulwer's son, attaché here) and Julian Fane (Secretary of the embassy), both great admirers of him, — and especially of the Biglow Papers, — they begged me

Letter from Vienna.

to send them the Mason and Slidell Idyl, but I would n't, — I don't think it is in English nature (although theirs is very cosmopolitan and liberal) to take such punishment and come up smiling. I would rather they got it in some other way, and then told me what they thought voluntarily.

"I have very pleasant relations with all the J. B.'s here. They are all friendly and well disposed to the North, — I speak of the embassy, which, with the ambassador and ——dress numbers eight or ten souls, — some of them very intellectual ones. There are no other J. B.'s here. I have no fear at present of foreign interference. We have got three or four months to do our work in, — a fair field and no favor. There is no question whatever that the Southern Commissioners have been thoroughly snubbed in London and Paris. There is to be a blockade debate in Parliament next week, but no bad consequences are to be apprehended. The Duke de Gramont (French Ambassador, and an intimate friend of the Emperor) told my wife last night that it was entirely false that the Emperor had ever urged the English government to break the blockade. 'Don't believe it, — don't believe a word of it,' he said. He has *always* held that language to me. He added that Prince Napoleon had just come out with a strong speech about us,—you

What Napoleon did not do.

Sect. XVII. 1862.

will see it, doubtless, before you get this letter,—but it has not yet reached us.

Letter from Vienna.

"Shall I say anything of Austria,—what can I say that would interest you? That's the reason why I hate to write. All my thoughts are in America. Do you care to know about the Archduke Ferdinand Maximilian, that shall be King hereafter of Mexico (if L. N. has his way)? He is next brother to the Emperor, but although I have had the honor of private audiences of many archdukes here, this one is a resident of Trieste.

The Archduke Maximilian.

His character.

"He is about thirty,—has an adventurous disposition,—some imagination,—a turn for poetry,—has voyaged a good deal about the world in the Austrian ship-of-war,—for in one respect he much resembles that unfortunate but anonymous ancestor of his, the King of Bohemia with the seven castles, who, according to Corporal Trim, had such a passion for navigation and sea-affairs, 'with never a seaport in all his dominions.' But now the present King of Bohemia has got the sway of Trieste, and is Lord High Admiral and Chief of the Marine Department. He has been much in Spain, also in South America,—I have read some travels, Reise Skizzen, of his—printed, not published. They are not without talent, and he ever and anon relieves his prose jog-trot by breaking into a canter of poetry. He adores bull-fights, and rather regrets the Inquisi-

His travels.

Letter from Vienna.

tion, and considers the Duke of Alva everything noble and chivalrous, and the most abused of men. It would do your heart good to hear his invocations to that deeply injured shade, and his denunciations of the ignorant and vulgar protestants who have defamed him. (N. B. Let me observe that the R. of the D. R. was not published until long after the Reise Skizzen were written.) Du armer Alva! weil du dem Willen deines Herrn unerschütterlich treu wast, weil die festbestimmten grundsätze der Regierung, etc, etc., etc. You can imagine the rest.

"Dear me! I wish I could get back to the sixteenth and seventeenth century. . . . . But alas! the events of the nineteenth are too engrossing.

"If Lowell cares to read this letter, will you allow me to 'make it over to him jointly,' as Captain Cuttle says. I wished to write to him, but I am afraid only you would tolerate my writing so much when I have nothing to say. If he would ever send me a line I should be infinitely obliged, and would quickly respond. We read the 'Washers of the Shroud' with fervid admiration.

The Saturday Club.

"Always remember me most sincerely to the Club, one and all. It touches me nearly when you assure me that I am not forgotten by them. To-morrow is *Saturday* and *the last of the month.** We are

* See Appendix A.

SECT. XVII. 1862.

going to dine with our Spanish colleague. But the first bumper of the Don's champagne I shall drain to the health of my Parker House friends."

Another letter from Vienna.

From another long letter dated August 31, 1862, I extract the following passages:—

"I quite agree in all that you said in your last letter. 'The imp of secession can't re-enter its mother's womb.' It is merely childish to talk of the Union 'as it was.' You might as well bring back the Saxon Heptarchy. But the Great Republic is destined to live and flourish, I can't doubt. .... Do you remember that wonderful scene in Faust in which Mephistopheles draws wine for the rabble with a gimlet out of the wooden table; and how it changes to fire as they drink it, and how they all go mad, draw their knives, grasp each other by the nose, and think they are cutting off bunches of grapes at every blow, and how foolish they all look when they awake from the spell and see how the Devil has been mocking them? It always seems to me a parable of the great Secession.

He has no doubt as to the result of the war.

"I repeat, I can't doubt as to the ultimate result. But I dare say we have all been much mistaken in our calculations as to time. Days, months, years, are nothing in history. *Men* die, *man* is immortal, practically, even on this earth. We are so impatient,—and we are always watching for the last scene of the tragedy. Now I humbly opine that the

Sect. XVII. 1862.

Letter from Vienna.

drop is only about falling on the first act, or perhaps only the prologue. This act or prologue will be called, in after days, War for the *status quo.*

"Such enthusiasm, heroism, and manslaughter as *status quo* could inspire, has, I trust, been not entirely in vain, but it has been proved insufficient.

"I firmly believe that when the slaveholders declared war on the United States Government they began a series of events that, in the logical chain of history, cannot come to a conclusion until the last vestige of slavery is gone. Looking at the whole field for a moment dispassionately, *objectively,* as the dear Teutonic philosophers say, and merely as an exhibition of phenomena, I cannot imagine any other issue. Everything else *may* happen. This alone *must* happen.

The struggle not a war, but a revolution.

"But after all this is n't a war. It is a revolution. It is n't strategists that are wanted so much as *believers.* In revolutions the men who win are those who are in earnest. Jeff and Stonewall and the other Devil-worshippers are in earnest, but it was not written in the book of fate that the slaveholders' rebellion should be vanquished by a pro-slavery general. History is never so illogical. No, the coming 'man on horseback' on our side must be a great strategist, with the soul of that insane lion, mad old John Brown, in his belly. That is your only Promethean recipe:—

SECT. XVII.
1862.

'et insani leonis
Vim stomacho apposuisse nostro.'

"I don't know why Horace runs so in my head this morning. . . . .

"There will be work enough for all — but I feel awfully fidgety just now about Port Royal and Hilton Head, and about affairs generally for the next three months. After that iron-clads and the new levies must make us invincible."

Another letter from Vienna.

In another letter, dated November 2, 1862, he expresses himself very warmly about his disappointment in the attitude of many of his old English friends with reference to our civil conflict. He had recently heard the details of the death of "the noble Wilder Dwight."

Refers to the death of Wilder Dwight.

"It is unnecessary," he says, "to say how deeply we were moved. I had the pleasure of knowing him well, and I always appreciated his energy, his manliness, and his intelligent cheerful heroism. I look back upon him now as a kind of heroic type of what a young New-Englander ought to be and was. I tell you that one of these days — after a generation of mankind has passed away — these youths will take their places in our history and be regarded by the young men and women now unborn with the admiration which the Philip Sidneys and the Max Piccolominis now inspire. After all, what was your Chevy Chace to stir blood with like a trumpet? What noble principle, what deathless interest, was there at stake? Nothing but a bloody fight between a lot of noble gamekeepers on one side and of noble poachers on the other. And because they fought well and hacked each other to pieces like devils, they have been heroes for centuries."

Letter from Vienna.

The letter was written in a very excited state of feeling, and runs over with passionate love of country and indignation at the want of sympathy with the cause of freedom which he had found in quarters where he had not expected such coldness or hostile tendencies.

From a letter dated Vienna, September 22, 1863.

". . . . When you wrote me last you said on general matters this: 'In a few days we shall get the news of the success or failure of the attacks on Port Hudson and Vicksburg. If both are successful, many will say that the whole matter is about settled.' You may suppose that when I got the great news I shook hands warmly with you in the spirit across the Atlantic. Day by day for so long we had been hoping to hear the fall of Vicksburg. At last when that little concentrated telegram came announcing Vicksburg and Gettysburg on the same day and in two lines, I found myself almost alone. . . . . There was nobody in the house to join in my huzzahs but my youngest infant. And my con-

Vicksburg and Gettysburg.

SECT. XVII. 1863.

Letter from Vienna.

duct very much resembled that of the excellent Philip II. when he heard the fall of Antwerp,—for I went to her door, screeching through the key-hole 'Vicksburg is ours!' just as that other père de famille, more potent, but I trust not more respectable than I, conveyed the news to his Infanta. (*Vide*, for the incident, an American work on the Netherlands, I. p. 263, and the authorities there cited.) It is contemptible on my part to speak thus frivolously of events which will stand out in such golden letters so long as America has a history, but I wanted to illustrate the yearning for sympathy which I felt. You who were among people grim and self-contained usually, who, I *trust*, were falling on each other's necks in the public streets, shouting, with tears in their eyes, and triumph in their hearts, can picture my isolation.

He has never faltered in his faith.

"I have never faltered in my faith, and in the darkest hours, when misfortunes seemed thronging most thickly upon us, I have never felt the want of anything to lean against; but I own I did feel like shaking hands with a few hundred people when I heard of our Fourth of July, 1863, work, and should like to have heard and joined in an American cheer or two. . . . .

Drought in in Austria.

". . . . I have not much to say of matters here to interest you. We have had an intensely hot, historically hot, and very long and very dry summer.

Sect. XVII. 1862.

I never knew before what a drought meant. In Hungary the suffering is great, and the people are killing the sheep to feed the pigs with the mutton. Here about Vienna the trees have been almost stripped of foliage ever since the end of August. There is no glory in the grass nor verdure in anything.

Letter from Vienna.

Great drought.

"In fact, we have nothing green here but the Archduke Max, who firmly believes that he is going forth to Mexico to establish an American empire, and that it is his divine mission to destroy the dragon of democracy and re-establish the true Church, the Right Divine, and all sorts of games. Poor young man! . . . .

Nothing green but poor Maximilian.

"Our information from home is to the 12th. Charleston seems to be in *articulo mortis,* but how forts nowadays seem to fly in the face of Scripture. Those founded on a rock and built of it fall easily enough under the rain of Parrotts and Dahlgrens, while the house built of sand seems to bid defiance to the storm."

The house on a rock and the house of sand.

In quoting from these confidential letters I have been restrained from doing full justice to their writer by the fact that he spoke with such entire freedom of persons as well as events. But if they could be read from beginning to end, no one could help feeling that his love for his own country, and passionate absorption of every thought in the strife upon which its existence as a nation depended, were his very life during all this agonizing period. He can think and talk of nothing else, or, if he turns for a moment to other subjects, he reverts to the one great central interest of "American politics," of which he says in one of the letters from which I have quoted, "There is nothing else *worth* thinking of in the world."

His patriotism not a defence against malevolence.

But in spite of his public record as the historian of the struggle for liberty and the champion of its defenders, and while every letter he wrote betrayed in every word the intensity of his patriotic feeling, he was not safe against the attacks of malevolence. A train laid by unseen hands was waiting for the spark to kindle it, and this came at last in the shape of a letter from an unknown individual, — a letter the existence of which ought never to have been a matter of official recognition.

XVIII.

Resignation of his Office. — Causes of his Resignation. (*1866 - 1867.*)

SECT. XVIII. 1866 - 1867.

It is a relief to me that just here, where I come to the first of two painful episodes in this brilliant and fortunate career, I can preface my statement with the generous words of one who speaks with authority of his predecessor in office.

Mr. Jay's tribute to Motley's memory.

The Hon. John Jay, Ex-Minister to Austria, in the Tribute to the memory of Motley read at a meeting of the New York Historical Society, wrote as follows: —

"In singular contrast to Mr. Motley's brilliant career as an historian stands the fact recorded in our diplomatic annals that he was twice forced from the service as one who had forfeited the confidence of the American Government. This Society, while he was living, recognized his fame as a statesman, diplomatist, and patriot, as belonging to America, and now that death has closed the career of Seward, Sumner, and Motley, it will be remembered that the great historian, twice humiliated, by orders from Washington, before the diplomacy and culture of Europe, appealed from the passions of the hour to the verdict of history.

Mr. Jay's characterization of Motley's despatches.

"Having succeeded Mr. Motley at Vienna some two years after his departure, I had occasion to read most of his despatches, which exhibited a mastery of the subjects of which they treated, with much of the clear perception, the scholarly and philosophic tone and decided judgment, which, supplemented by his picturesque description, full of life and color, have given character to his histories. They are features which might well have served to extend the remark of Madame de Staël that a great historian is almost a statesman. I can speak also from my own observation of the reputation which Motley left in the Austrian capital. Notwithstanding the decision with which, under the direction of Mr. Seward, he had addressed the minister of Foreign Affairs, Count Mensdorff, afterwards the Prince Diedrickstein, protesting against the departure of an Austrian force of one thousand volunteers, who were about to embark for Mexico in aid of the ill-fated Maximilian, — a protest which at the last moment arrested the project, — Mr. Motley and his amiable family were always spoken of in terms of cordial regard and respect by members of the imperial family and those eminent statesmen, Count de Beust and Count Andrassy. His death, I am sure, is mourned to-day by the

How he was regarded at Vienna.

representatives of the historic names of Austria and Hungary, and by the surviving diplomats then residing near the Court of Vienna, wherever they may still be found, headed by their venerable Doyen, the Baron de Heckéren."

SECT. XVIII. 1866.

Story of Mr. Motley's resignation.

The story of Mr. Motley's resignation of his office and its acceptance by the Government is this.

The M'Crackin letter.

The President of the United States, Andrew Johnson, received a letter professing to be written from the Hotel Meurice, Paris, dated October 23, 1866, and signed "George W. M'Crackin, of New York." This letter was filled with accusations directed against various public agents, ministers, and consuls, representing the United States in different countries. Its language was coarse, its assertions were improbable, its spirit that of the lowest of party scribblers. It was bitter against New England, especially so against Massachusetts, and it singled out Motley for the most particular abuse. I think it is still questioned whether there was any such person as the one named, — at any rate, it bore the characteristic marks of those vulgar anonymous communications which rarely receive any attention unless they are important enough to have the police set on the track of the writer to find his rathole, if possible. A paragraph in the Daily Adver-

SECT. XVIII. 1866.

tiser of June 7, 1869 quotes from a Western paper a story to the effect that one *William R.* M'Cracken, who had recently died at ——, confessed to having written the M'Crackin letter. Motley, he said, had snubbed him and refused to lend him money. "He appears to have been a Bohemian of the lowest order." Between such authorship and the anonymous there does not seem to be much to choose. But the dying confession sounds in my ears as decidedly apocryphal. As for the letter, I had rather characterize it than reproduce it. It is an offence to decency and a disgrace to the national record on which it is found.

Its authorship.

What should have been done with it.

This letter of "George W. M'Crackin" passed into the hands of Mr. Seward, the Secretary of State. Most gentlemen, I think, would have destroyed it on the spot, as it was not fit for the waste-basket. Some, more cautious, might have smothered it among the piles of their private communications. If any notice was taken of it, one would say that a private note to each of the gentlemen attacked might have warned him that there were malicious eavesdroppers about, ready to catch up any careless expression he might let fall and make a scandalous report of it to his detriment.

What was done with it.

The Secretary, acquiescing without resistance in a suggestion of the President, saw fit to address a formal note to several of the gentlemen mentioned

The M'Crackin letter.

in the M'Crackin letter, repeating some of its offensive expressions, and requesting those officials to deny or confirm the report that they had uttered them.

A gentleman who is asked whether he has spoken in a "malignant" or "offensive" manner, whether he has "railed violently and shamefully" against the President of the United States, or against anybody else, might well wonder who would address such a question to the humblest citizen not supposed to be wanting in a common measure of self-respect. A gentleman holding an important official station in a foreign country, receiving a letter containing such questions, signed by the Prime Minister of his government, if he did not think himself imposed upon by a forgery, might well consider himself outraged. It was a letter of this kind which was sent by the Secretary of State to the Minister Plenipotentiary to the Empire of Austria. Not quite all the vulgar insolence of the M'Crackin letter was repeated. Mr. Seward did not ask Mr. Motley to deny or confirm the assertion of the letter that he was a "thorough flunky" and "un-American functionary." But he did insult him with various questions suggested by the anonymous letter,—questions that must have been felt as an indignity by the most thick-skinned of battered politicians.

Mr. Seward questions Mr. Motley about it.

Mr. Motley was very sensitive, very high-spirited,

Sect. XVIII. 1866.

very impulsive, very patriotic, and singularly truthful. The letter of Mr. Seward to such a man was like a buffet on the cheek of an unarmed officer. It stung like the thrust of a stiletto. It roused a resentment that could not find any words to give it expression. He could not wait to turn the insult over in his mind, to weigh the exact amount of affront in each question, to take counsel, to sleep over it, and reply to it with diplomatic measure and suavity. One hour had scarcely elapsed before his answer was written. As to his feelings as an American, he appeals to his record. This might have shown that if he erred it was on the side of enthusiasm and extravagant expressions of reverence for the American people during the heroic years just passed. He denounces the accusations as pitiful fabrications and vile calumny. He blushes that such charges could have been uttered; he is deeply wounded that Mr. Seward could have listened to such falsehood. He does not hesitate to say what his opinions are with reference to home questions, and especially to that of reconstruction.

He replies immediately.

He denies and denounces the accusations.

"These opinions," he says, "in the privacy of my own household, and to occasional American visitors, I have not concealed. The great question now presenting itself for solution demands the conscientious scrutiny of every American who loves his country and believes in the human progress of which that country is one of the foremost representatives. I have never thought, during my residence at Vienna, that because I have the honor of being a public servant of the American people I am deprived of the right of discussing within my own walls the gravest subjects that can interest freemen. A minister of the United States does not cease to be a citizen of the United States, as deeply interested as others in all that relates to the welfare of his country."

"Interviewers."

Among the "occasional American visitors" spoken of above must have been some of those self-appointed or hired agents called "interviewers," who do for the American public what the Venetian spies did for the Council of Ten, what the familiars of the Inquisition did for the priesthood, who invade every public man's privacy, who listen at every key-hole, who tamper with every guardian of secrets; purveyors to the insatiable appetite of a public which must have a slain reputation to devour with its breakfast, as the monster of antiquity called regularly for his tribute of a spotless virgin.

The "interviewer" has his use, undoubtedly, and often instructs and amuses his public with gossip they could not otherwise listen to. He serves the politician by repeating the artless and unstudied remarks which fall from his lips in a conversation which the reporter has been invited to take notes of.

SECT. XVIII. 1866.

"Interviewers," their use and their mischief-making.

He tickles the author's vanity by showing him off as he sits in his library unconsciously uttering the engaging items of self-portraiture which, as he well knows, are to be given to the public in next week's illustrated paper. The feathered end of his shaft titillates harmlessly enough, but too often the arrowhead is crusted with a poison worse than the Indian gets by mingling the wolf's gall with the rattlesnake's venom. No man is safe whose unguarded threshold the mischief-making questioner has crossed. The more unsuspecting, the more frank, the more courageous, the more social is the subject of his vivisection, the more easily does he get at his vital secrets, if he has any to be extracted. No man is safe if the hearsay reports of his conversation are to be given to the public without his own careful revision. When we remember that a proof-text bearing on the mighty question of the future life, words of supreme significance, uttered as they were in the last hour, and by the lips to which we listen as to none other, — that this text depends for its interpretation on the position of a single comma, we can readily see what wrong may be done by the unintentional blunder of the most conscientious reporter. But too frequently it happens that the careless talk of an honest and high-minded man only reaches the public after filtering through the drain of some reckless hireling's memory, — one who has played so long with other men's characters and good name that he forgets they have any value except to fill out his morning paragraphs.

Whether the author of the scandalous letter which it was disgraceful to the Government to recognize was a professional interviewer or only a malicious amateur, or whether he was a paid "spotter," sent by some jealous official to report on the foreign ministers as is sometimes done in the case of conductors of city horse-cars, or whether the dying miscreant before mentioned told the truth, cannot be certainly known. But those who remember Mr. Hawthorne's account of his consular experiences at Liverpool are fully aware to what intrusions and impertinences and impositions our national representatives in other countries are subjected. Those fellow-citizens who "often came to the consulate in parties of half a dozen or more, on no business whatever, but merely to subject their public servant to a rigid examination, and see how he was getting on with his duties," may very possibly have included among them some such mischief-maker as the author of the odious letter which received official recognition. Mr. Motley had spoken in one of his histories of "a set of venomous familiars who glided through every chamber and coiled themselves at every fireside." He little thought

What public servants are exposed to.

Mr. Hawthorne's experience.

SECT. XVIII. 1866.

that under his own roof he himself was to be the victim of an equally base espionage.

The questions addressed to Mr. Motley an insult.

It was an insult on the part of the Government to have sent Mr. Motley such a letter with such questions as were annexed to it. No very exact rule can be laid down as to the manner in which an insult shall be dealt with. Something depends on temperament, and his was of the warmer complexion. His first impulse, he says, was to content himself with a flat denial of the truth of the accusations. But his scrupulous honesty compelled him to make a plain statement of his opinions, and to avow the fact that he had made no secret of them in conversation under conditions where he had a right to speak freely of matters quite apart from his official duties. His answer to the accusation was denial of its charges; his reply to the insult was his resignation.

He resigns his office.

It may be questioned whether this was the wisest course, but wisdom is often disconcerted by an indignity, and even a meek Christian may forget to turn the other cheek after receiving the first blow until the natural man has asserted himself by a retort in kind. But the wrong was committed; his resignation was accepted; the vulgar letter, not fit to be spread out on these pages, is enrolled in the records of the nation, and the first deep wound was inflicted on the proud spirit of one whose renown had shed lustre on the whole country.

His resignation accepted.

SECT. XVIII. 1866.

That the burden of this wrong may rest where it belongs, I quote the following statement from Mr. Jay's paper, already referred to.

Mr. Seward cleared by a "reliable authority."

"It is due to the memory of Mr. Seward to say, and there would seem now no further motive for concealing the truth, that I was told in Europe, on what I regarded as reliable authority, that there was reason to believe that on the receipt of Mr. Motley's resignation Mr. Seward had written to him declining to accept it, and that this letter, by a telegraphic order of President Johnson, had been arrested in the hands of a despatch agent before its delivery to Mr. Motley, and that the curt letter of the 18th of April had been substituted in its stead."

Mr. Seward not cleared, but defended by Hon. John Bigelow.

The Hon. John Bigelow, late Minister to France, has published an article in the International Review for July – August, 1878, in which he defends his late friend Mr. Seward's action in this matter at the expense of the President, Mr. Andrew Johnson, and not without inferences unfavorable to the discretion of Mr. Motley. Many readers will think that the simple record of Mr. Seward's unresisting acquiescence in the action of the President is far from being to his advantage. I quote from his own conversation as carefully reported by his friend Mr. Bigelow. "Mr. Johnson was in a state of intense irritation, and more or less suspicious of

SECT. XVIII. 1867.

Mr. Johnson intensely irritated and suspicious of everybody.

everybody about him." "Instead of throwing the letter into the fire," the President handed it to him, the Secretary, and suggested answering it, and without a word, so far as appears, he simply answered, "Certainly, sir." Again, the Secretary having already written to Mr. Motley that "his answer was satisfactory," the President, on reaching the last paragraph of Mr. Motley's letter, in which he begged respectfully to resign his post, "without waiting to learn what Mr. Seward had done or proposed to do, exclaimed, with a not unnatural asperity, 'Well, let him go,' and 'on hearing this,' said Mr. Seward, laughing, 'I did not read my despatch.'" Many persons will think that the counsel for the defence has stated the plaintiff's case so strongly that there is nothing left for him but to show his ingenuity and his friendship for the late Secretary in a hopeless argument. At any rate, Mr. Seward appears not to have made the slightest effort to protect Mr. Motley against his coarse and jealous chief at two critical moments, and though his own continuance in office may have been more important to the State than that of the Vicar of Bray was to the Church, he ought to have risked something, as it seems to me, to shield such a patriot, such a gentleman, such a scholar, from ignoble treatment; he ought to have been as ready to guard Mr. Motley from wrong as Mr. Bigelow has shown him-

Mr. Seward compliant.

self to shield Mr. Seward from reproach, and his task, if more delicate, was not more difficult. I am willing to accept Mr. Bigelow's loyal and honorable defence of his friend's memory as the best that could be said for Mr. Seward, but the best defence in this case is little better than an impeachment. As for Mr. Johnson, he had held the weapon of the most relentless of the Parcæ so long that his suddenly clipping the thread of a foreign minister's tenure of office in a fit of jealous anger is not at all surprising.

Thus finished Mr. Motley's long and successful diplomatic service at the Court of Austria. He may have been judged hasty in resigning his place; he may have committed himself in expressing his opinions too strongly before strangers, whose true character as spies and eavesdroppers he was too high-minded to suspect. But no caution could have protected him against a slanderer who hated the place he came from, the company he kept, the name he had made famous, to whom his very look and bearing — such as belong to a gentleman of natural refinement and good breeding — must have been a personal grievance and an unpardonable offence.

Mr. Motley the victim of a slanderer.

I will add, in illustration of what has been said, and as showing his feeling with reference to the matter, an extract from a letter to me from Vienna, dated the 12th of March, 1867.

SECT. XVIII. 1867.

His letter to me about the M'Crackin business.

" . . . As so many friends and so many strangers have said so much that is gratifying to me in public and private on this very painful subject, it would be like affectation, in writing to so old a friend as you, not to touch upon it. I shall confine myself, however, to one fact, which, so far as I know, may be new to you.

"Geo. W. M'Cracken is a man and a name utterly unknown to me.

"With the necessary qualification which every man who values truth must make when asserting such a negation, — viz., to the very best of my memory and belief, — I never set eyes on him nor heard of him until now, in the whole course of my life. Not a member of my family or of the legation has the faintest recollection of any such person. I am quite convinced that he never saw me nor heard the sound of my voice. That his letter was a tissue of vile calumnies, shameless fabrications, and unblushing and contemptible falsehoods, — by whomsoever uttered, — I have stated in a reply to what ought never to have been an official letter. No man can regret more than I do that such a correspondence is enrolled in the capital among American State Papers. I shall not trust myself to speak of the matter. It has been a sufficiently public scandal."

XIX.

Last Two Volumes of the "History of the United Netherlands."—General Criticisms of Dutch Scholars on Motley's Historical Works. (*1867-1868.*)

SECT. XIX. 1867-1868.

His literary plans.

In his letter to me of March 12, 1867, just cited, Mr. Motley writes: —

"My two concluding volumes of the United Netherlands are passing rapidly through the press. Indeed, Volume III. is entirely printed and a third of Volume IV.

"If I live ten years longer I shall have probably written the natural sequel to the first two works, — viz., the Thirty Years' War. After that I shall cease to scourge the public.

"I don't know whether my last two volumes are good or bad — I only know that they are true — but that need n't make them amusing.

"Alas — one never knows when one becomes a bore."

Last two volumes of the History of the United Netherlands.

In 1868 the two concluding volumes of the History of the Netherlands were published at the same time in London and in New York. The events

SECT. XIX. 1868.

History of the United Netherlands.

described and the characters delineated in these two volumes had, perhaps, less peculiar interest for English and American readers than some of those which had lent attraction to the preceding ones. There was no scene like the siege of Antwerp, no story like that of the Spanish Armada. There were no names that sounded to our ears like those of Sir Philip Sidney and Leicester and Amy Robsart. But the main course of his narrative flowed on with the same breadth and depth of learning and the same brilliancy of expression. The monumental work continued as nobly as it had begun. The facts had been slowly, quietly gathered one by one, like pebbles from the empty channel of a brook.

His style.

The style was fluent, impetuous, abundant, impatient, as it were, at times, and leaping the sober boundaries prescribed to it, like the torrent which rushes through the same channel when the rains have filled it. Thus there was matter for criticism in his use of language. He was not always careful in the construction of his sentences. He introduced expressions now and then into his vocabulary which reminded one of his earlier literary efforts. He used stronger language at times than was necessary, coloring too highly, shading too deeply in his pictorial delineations. To come to the matter of his narrative, it must be granted that not every reader will care to follow him through all the details of diplomatic intrigues which he has with such industry and sagacity extricated from the old manuscripts in which they had long lain hidden. But we turn a few pages and we come to one of those descriptions which arrest us at once and show him in his power and brilliancy as a literary artist. His characters move before us with the features of life; we can see Elizabeth, or Philip, or Maurice, not as a name connected with events, but as a breathing and acting human being, to be loved or hated, admired or despised as if he or she were our contemporary. That all his judgments would not be accepted as final we might easily anticipate; he could not help writing more or less as a partisan, but he was a partisan on the side of freedom in politics and religion, of human nature as against every form of tyranny, secular or priestly, of noble manhood wherever he saw it as against meanness and violence and imposture, whether clad in the soldier's mail or the emperor's purple. His sternest critics, and even these admiring ones, were yet to be found among those who with fundamental beliefs at variance with his own followed him in his long researches among the dusty annals of the past.

History of the United Netherlands.

His characters.

His judgments.

The work of the learned M. Groen van Prinsterer (" Maurice et Barnevelt, Étude Historique. Utrecht, 1875 "), devoted expressly to the revision and correction of what the author considers the erroneous

M. Groen van Prinsterer.

SECT. XIX. 1868.

views of Mr. Motley on certain important points, bears, notwithstanding, such sincere and hearty tribute to his industry, his acquisitions, his brilliant qualities as a historian, that some extracts from it will be read, I think, with interest.

"My first interview, more than twenty years ago, with Mr. Lothrop Motley, has left an indelible impression on my memory.

Account of his first interview with Mr. Motley.

"It was the 8th of August, 1853. A note is handed me from our eminent Archivist Bakhuizen van den Brink. It informs me that I am to receive a visit from an American, who, having been struck by the analogies between the United Provinces and the United States, between Washington and the founder of our independence, has interrupted his diplomatic career to write the life of William the First; that he has already given proof of ardor and perseverance, having worked in libraries and among collections of manuscripts, and that he is coming to pursue his studies at the Hague.

"While I am surprised and delighted with this intelligence, I am informed that Mr. Motley himself is waiting for my answer. My eagerness to make the acquaintance of such an associate in my sympathies and my labors may be well imagined. But how shall I picture my surprise, in presently discovering that this unknown and indefatigable

M. Groen van Prinsterer.

fellow-worker has really read, I say read and re-read our *Quartos*, our *Folios*, the enormous volumes of *Bor*, of *van Meteren*, besides a multitude of books, of pamphlets, and even of unedited documents. Already he is familiar with the events, the changes of condition, the characteristic details of the life of his and my hero. Not only is he acquainted with my Archives, but it seems as if there was nothing in this voluminous collection of which he was ignorant. . . . .

"In sending me the last volume of his History of the Foundation of the Republic of the Netherlands, Mr. Motley wrote to me: 'Without the help of the Archives I could never have undertaken the difficult task I had set myself, and you will have seen at least from my numerous citations that I have made a sincere and conscientious study of them.' Certainly in reading such a testimonial I congratulated myself on the excellent fruit of my labors, but the gratitude expressed to me by Mr. Motley was sincerely reciprocated. The Archives are a scientific collection, and my Manual of National History, written in Dutch, hardly gets beyond the limits of my own country. And here is a stranger, become our compatriot in virtue of the warmth of his sympathies, who has accomplished what was not in my power. By the detail and the charm of his narrative, by the matter and form of

SECT. XIX. 1868.

M. Groen van Prinsterer.

a work which the universality of the English language and numerous translations were to render cosmopolitan, Mr. Motley, like that other illustrious historian, Prescott, lost to science by too early death, has popularized in both hemispheres the sublime devotion of the Prince of Orange, the exceptional and providential destinies of my country, and the benedictions of the Eternal for all those who trust in Him and tremble only at his Word."

Historians and archivists.

The old Dutch scholar differs in many important points from Mr. Motley, as might be expected from his creed and his life-long pursuits. This I shall refer to in connection with Motley's last work, "John of Barneveld." An historian among archivists and annalists reminds one of Sir John Lubbock in the midst of his ant-hills. Undoubtedly he disturbs the ants in their praiseworthy industry, much as his attentions may flatter them. Unquestionably the ants (if their means of expressing themselves were equal to their apparent intellectual ability) could teach him many things that he has overlooked and correct him in many mistakes. But the ants will labor ingloriously without an observer to chronicle their doings, and the archivists and annalists will pile up facts forever like so many articulates or mollusks or radiates, until the vertebrate historian comes with his generalizing ideas, his beliefs, his prejudices, his idiosyncrasies of all kinds, and brings the facts into a more or less imperfect, but still organic series of relations. The history which is not open to adverse criticism is worth little, except as material, for it is written without taking cognizance of those higher facts about which men must differ; of which Guizot writes as follows, as quoted in the work of M. Groen van Prinsterer himself.

M. Guizot on *facts*.

"It is with *facts* that our minds are exercised, it has nothing but facts as its materials, and when it discovers general laws these laws are themselves facts which it determines. . . . . In the study of *facts* the intelligence may allow itself to be crushed; it may lower, narrow, materialize itself; it may come to believe that there are no facts except those which strike us at the first glance, which come close to us, which fall, as we say, under our senses: a great and gross error; there are *remote facts*, immense, obscure, sublime, very difficult to reach, to observe, to describe, and which are not any less *facts* for these reasons, and which man is not less obliged to study and to know; and if he fails to recognize them or forgets them, his thought will be prodigiously abased, and all his ideas carry the stamp of this deterioration."

In that higher region of facts which belongs to the historian, whose task it is to interpret as well

SECT. XIX. 1868.

Testimony of Dutch critics to Motley's sincerity and truthfulness.

as to transcribe, Mr. Motley showed, of course, the political and religious school in which he had been brought up. Every man has a right to his "personal equation" of prejudice, and Mr. Motley, whose ardent temperament gave life to his writings, betrayed his sympathies in the disputes of which he told the story, in a way to insure sharp criticism from those of a different way of thinking. Thus it is that in the work of M. Groen van Prinsterer, from which I have quoted, he is considered as having been betrayed into error, while his critic recognizes "his manifest desire to be scrupulously impartial and truth-telling." And M. Fruin, another of his Dutch critics, says, "His sincerity, his perspicacity, the accuracy of his laborious researches, are incontestable."

Some of the criticisms of Dutch scholars will be considered in the pages which deal with his last work, "The Life of John of Barneveld."

XX.

Visit to America. — Residence at No. 2 Park Street, Boston. — Address on the coming Presidential Election. — Address on the Historic Progress of American Democracy. — Appointed Minister to England. (*1868-1869.*)

SECT. XX. 1868.

Return to Boston.

In June, 1868, Mr. Motley returned with his family to Boston, and established himself in the house No. 2 Park Street. During his residence here he entered a good deal into society, and entertained many visitors in a most hospitable and agreeable way.

Address before the Parker Fraternity.

On the 20th of October, 1868, he delivered an address before the Parker Fraternity, in the Music Hall, by special invitation. Its title was "Four questions for the people, at the Presidential Election." This was of course what is commonly called an electioneering speech, but a speech full of noble sentiments and eloquent expression. Here are two of its paragraphs: —

"Certainly there have been bitterly contested elections in this country before. Party spirit is always rife, and in such vivid, excitable, disputa-

SECT. XX. 1868.

Address before the Parker Fraternity.

tious communities as ours are, and I trust always will be, it is the very soul of freedom. To those who reflect upon the means and end of popular government, nothing seems more stupid than in grand generalities to deprecate party spirit. Why, government by parties and through party machinery is the only possible method by which a free government can accomplish the purpose of its existence. The old republics of the past may be said to have fallen, not because of party spirit, but because there was no adequate machinery by which party spirit could develop itself with facility and regularity.

". . . . And if our Republic be true to herself, the future of the human race is assured by our example. No sweep of overwhelming armies, no ponderous treatises on the rights of man, no hymns to liberty, though set to martial music and resounding with the full diapason of a million human throats, can exert so persuasive an influence as does the spectacle of a great republic, occupying a quarter of the civilized globe, and governed quietly and sagely by the people itself."

A large portion of this address is devoted to the proposition that it is just and reasonable to pay our debts rather than to repudiate them, and that the nation is as much bound to be honest as is the individual. "It is an awful thing," he says, "that this should be a question at all," but it was one of the points on which the election turned, for all that.

Address before the Parker Fraternity.

In his advocacy of the candidate with whom and the government of which he became the head, his relations became afterwards so full of personal antagonism, he spoke as a man of his ardent nature might be expected to speak on such an occasion. No one doubts that his admiration of General Grant's career was perfectly sincere, and no one at the present day can deny that the great Captain stood before the historian with such a record as one familiar with the deeds of heroes and patriots might well consider as entitling him to the honors too often grudged to the living to be wasted on the dead. The speaker only gave voice to the widely prevailing feelings which had led to his receiving the invitation to speak. The time was one which called for outspoken utterance, and there was not a listener whose heart did not warm as he heard the glowing words in which the speaker recorded the noble achievements of the soldier who must in so many ways have reminded him of his favorite character, William the Silent.

Address before the New York Historical Society.

On the 16th of December of this same year, 1868, Mr. Motley delivered an address before the New York Historical Society, on the occasion of the sixty-fourth anniversary of its foundation. The

Sect. XX.
1868.

Address before the New York Historical Society.

president of the society, Mr. Hamilton Fish, introduced the speaker as one "whose name belongs to no single country, and to no single age. As a statesman and diplomatist and patriot, he belongs to America; as a scholar, to the world of letters; as a historian, all ages will claim him in the future."

His subject was "Historic Progress and American Democracy." The discourse is, to use his own words, "a rapid sweep through the eons and the centuries," illustrating the great truth of the development of the race from its origin to the time in which we are living. It is a long distance from the planetary fact of the obliquity of the equator, which gave the earth its alternation of seasons, and rendered the history, if not the existence of man and of civilization a possibility, to the surrender of General Lee under the apple-tree at Appomattox Court-House. No one but a scholar familiar with the course of history could have marshalled such a procession of events into a connected and intelligible sequence. It is indeed a flight rather than a march; the reader is borne along as on the wings of a soaring poem, and sees the rising and decaying empires of history beneath him as a bird of passage marks the succession of cities and wilds and deserts as he keeps pace with the sun in his journey. Its eloquence, its patriotism, its crowded illustrations, drawn from vast resources of knowledge, its epigrammatic axioms, its occasional pleasantries, are all characteristic of the writer.

Vote of thanks. Mr. Verplanck.

Mr. Gulian C. Verplanck, the venerable senior member of the society, proposed the vote of thanks to Mr. Motley with words of warm commendation.

Mr. Bryant.

Mr. William Cullen Bryant rose and said: —

"I take great pleasure in seconding the resolution which has just been read. The eminent historian of the Dutch Republic, who has made the story of its earlier days as interesting as that of Athens and Sparta, and who has infused into the narrative the generous glow of his own genius, has the highest of titles to be heard with respectful attention by the citizens of a community which, in its origin, was an offshoot of that renowned republic. And cheerfully has that title been recognized, as the vast audience assembled here to-night, in spite of the storm, fully testifies; and well has our illustrious friend spoken of the growth of civilization and of the improvement in the condition of mankind, both in the Old World — the institutions of which he has so lately observed — and in the country which is proud to claim him as one of her children."

Appointed Minister to England.

Soon after the election of General Grant, Mr. Motley received the appointment of Minister to England. That the position was one which was in many respects most agreeable to him cannot be

SECT. XX. 1868-1869.

doubted. Yet it was not with unmingled feelings of satisfaction, not without misgivings which warned him but too truly of the dangers about to encompass him, that he accepted the place. He writes to me on April 16, 1869: —

His feelings about his appointment.

". . . . I feel anything but exultation at present, — rather the opposite sensation. I feel that I am placed higher than I deserve, and at the same time that I am taking greater responsibilities than ever were assumed by me before. *You* will be indulgent to my mistakes and shortcomings, — and who can expect to avoid them? But the world will be cruel. and the times are threatening. I shall do my best — but the best may be poor enough — and keep 'a heart for any fate.'"

XXI.

Recall from the English Mission. — Its Alleged and its Probable Reasons. (*1869–1870.*)

Sect. XXI. 1869 - 1870.

The English Mission.

The misgivings thus expressed to me in confidence, natural enough in one who had already known what it is to fall on evil days and evil tongues, were but too well justified by after events. I could have wished to leave untold the story of the English mission, an episode in Motley's life full of heart-burnings, and long to be regretted as a passage of American history. But his living appeal to my indulgence comes to me from his grave as a call for his defence, however little needed, at least as a part of my tribute to his memory. It is little needed, because the case is clear enough to all intelligent readers of our diplomatic history, and because his cause has been amply sustained by others in many ways better qualified than myself to do it justice. The task is painful, for if a wrong was done him it must be laid at the doors of those whom the nation has delighted to honor and whose services no error of judgment or feeling or conduct can ever induce us to forget. If he confessed him-

SECT. XXI. 1869-1870.

self liable, like the rest of us, to mistakes and shortcomings, we must remember that the great officers of the Government who decreed his downfall were not less the subjects of human infirmity.

His nomination unanimously confirmed.

The outline to be filled up is this: A new administration had just been elected. The "Alabama Treaty," negotiated by Motley's predecessor, Mr. Reverdy Johnson, had been rejected by the Senate. The minister was recalled, and Motley, nominated without opposition and unanimously confirmed by the Senate, was sent to England in his place. He was welcomed most cordially on his arrival at Liverpool, and replied in a similar strain of good feeling, expressing the same kindly sentiments which may be found in his instructions. Soon after arriving in London he had a conversation with Lord Clarendon, the British Foreign Secretary, of which he sent a full report to his own government. While the reported conversation was generally approved of in the government's despatch acknowledging it, it was hinted that some of its expressions were stronger than were required by the instructions, and that one of its points was not conveyed in precise conformity with the President's view. The criticism was very gently worded, and the despatch closed with a somewhat guarded paragraph repeating the Government's approbation.

He goes to England.

Addresses at Liverpool.

Conversation with Lord Clarendon.

Some expressions objected to.

This was the first offence alleged against Mr.

Motley. The second ground of complaint was that he had shown written minutes of this conversation to Lord Clarendon to obtain his confirmation of its exactness, and that he had — as he said, inadvertently — omitted to make mention to the Government of this circumstance until some weeks after the time of the interview.

Showed minutes of conversation to Lord Clarendon.

He was requested to explain to Lord Clarendon that a portion of his presentation and treatment of the subject discussed at the interview immediately after his arrival was disapproved by the Secretary of State, and he did so in a written communication, in which he used the very words employed by Mr. Fish in his criticism of the conversation with Lord Clarendon.

Requested to explain, and does so.

An alleged mistake; a temperate criticism, coupled with a general approval; a rectification of the mistake criticised. All this within the first two months of Mr. Motley's official residence in London.

All this within first two months of his official residence.

No further fault was found with him, so far as appears, in the discharge of his duties, to which he must have devoted himself faithfully, for he writes to me, under the date of December 27, 1870: "I have worked harder in the discharge of this mission than I ever did in my life." This from a man whose working powers astonished the old Dutch archivist, Groen van Prinsterer, means a good deal.

More than a year had elapsed since the inter-

SECT. XXI. 1869-1870.

Instructions of September 25, 1869.

view with Lord Clarendon, which had been the subject of criticism. In the mean time a paper of instructions was sent to Motley, dated September 25, 1869, in which the points in the report of his interview which had been found fault with are so nearly covered by similar expressions, that there seemed no real ground left for difference between the Government and the minister. Whatever overstatement there had been, these new instructions would imply that the Government was now ready to go quite as far as the minister had gone, and in some points to put the case still more strongly. Everything was going on quietly. Important business had been transacted, with no sign of distrust or discontent on the part of the Government as regarded Motley. Whatever mistake he was thought to have committed was condoned by amicable treatment, neutralized by the virtual indorsement of the Government in the instructions of the 25th of September, and obsolete as a ground of quarrel by lapse of time. The question about which the misunderstanding, if such it deserves to be called, had taken place, was no longer a possible source of disagreement, as it had long been settled that the Alabama case should only be opened again at the suggestion of the British Government, and that it should be transferred to Washington whenever that suggestion should again bring it up for consideration.

No sign of distrust of him or discontent with him.

Such was the aspect of affairs at the American Legation in London. No foreign minister felt more secure in his place than Mr. Motley. "I thought myself," he says in the letter of December 27, "entirely in the confidence of my own government, and I know that I had the thorough confidence and the friendship of the leading personages in England." All at once, on the first of July, 1870, a letter was written by the Secretary of State, requesting him to resign. This gentle form of violence is well understood in the diplomatic service. Horace Walpole says, speaking of Lady Archibald Hamilton: "They have civilly asked her and grossly forced her to ask civilly to go away, which she has done, with a pension of twelve hundred a year." Such a request is like the embrace of the "virgin" in old torture-chambers. She is robed in soft raiment, but beneath it are the knife-blades which are ready to lacerate and kill the victim, if he awaits the pressure of the machinery already in motion.

All at once he is requested to resign.

Mr. Motley knew well what was the logical order in an official execution, and saw fit to let the Government work its will upon him as its servant. In November he was recalled.

He does not resign, and is recalled.

The recall of a minister under such circumstances is an unusual if not an unprecedented occurrence. The government which appoints a citizen to represent the country at a foreign court assumes a very serious obligation to him. The next administration may turn him out and nothing will be thought of it. He may be obliged to ask for his passports and leave all at once if war is threatened between his own country and that which he represents. He may, of course, be recalled for gross misconduct. But his dismissal is a very serious matter to him personally, and not to be thought of on the ground of passion or caprice. Marriage is a simple business, but divorce is a very different thing. The world wants to know the reason of it; the law demands its justification. It was a great blow to Mr. Motley, a cause of indignation to those who were interested in him, a surprise and a mystery to the world in general.

Dismissal under these circumstances a great injury.

When he, his friends, and the public, all startled by this unexpected treatment, looked to find an explanation of it, one was found which seemed to many quite sufficient. Mr. Sumner had been prominent among those who had favored his appointment. A very serious breach had taken place between the President and Mr. Sumner on the important San Domingo question. It was a quarrel, in short, neither more nor less, at least so far as the President was concerned. The proposed San Domingo treaty had just been rejected by the Senate, on the thirtieth day of June, and immedi-

Explanation sought and supposed to be found in his relations with Mr. Sumner.

ately thereupon, — the very next day, — the letter requesting Mr. Motley's resignation was issued by the Executive. This fact was interpreted as implying something more than a mere coincidence. It was thought that Sumner's friend, who had been supported by him as a candidate for high office, who shared many of his political ideas and feelings, who was his intimate associate, his fellow-townsman, his companion in scholarship and cultivation, his sympathetic co-laborer in many ways, had been accounted and dealt with as the ally of an enemy, and that the shaft which struck to the heart of the sensitive Envoy had glanced from the *æs triplex* of the obdurate Senator.

A "coincidence" or something more.

Mr. Motley wrote a letter to the Secretary of State immediately after his recall, in which he reviewed his relations with the Government from the time of his taking office, and showed that no sufficient reason could be assigned for the treatment to which he had been subjected. He referred finally to the public rumor which assigned the President's hostility to his friend Sumner, growing out of the San Domingo treaty question, as the cause of his own removal, and to the coincidence between the dates of the rejection of the treaty and his dismissal, with an evident belief that these two occurrences were connected by something more than accident.

He writes to the Secretary of State and refers to the rumors as the cause of his recall.

To this, a reply was received from the Secretary

Sect. XXI. 1869-1870.

of State's office, signed by Mr. Fish, but so objectionable in its tone and expressions that it has been generally doubted whether the paper could claim anything more of the Secretary's hand than his signature. It travelled back to the old record of the conversation with Lord Clarendon, more than a year and a half before, took up the old exceptions, warmed them over into grievances, and joined with them whatever the *captatores verborum,* not extinct since Daniel Webster's time, could add to their number. This was the letter which was rendered so peculiarly offensive by a most undignified comparison which startled every well-bred reader. No answer was possible to such a letter, and the matter rested until the death of Mr. Motley caused it to be brought up once more for judgment.

The reply to Mr. Motley.

No answer possible to such a letter.

The Honorable John Jay, in his tribute to the memory of Mr. Motley, read at a meeting of the New York Historical Society, vindicated his character against the attacks of the late Executive in such a way as to leave an unfavorable impression as to the course of the Government. Objection was made on this account to placing the tribute upon the minutes of the Society. This led to a publication by Mr. Jay, entitled "Motley's Appeal to History," in which the propriety of the Society's action is questioned, and the wrong done to him insisted upon and further illustrated.

Hon. John Jay and the New York Historical Society.

Mr. Jay's publication, "Motley's Appeal to History."

Mr. Jay speaks with authority for his predecessor.

The defence could not have fallen into better hands. Bearing a name which is, in itself, a title to the confidence of the American people, a diplomatist familiar with the rights, the customs, the traditions, the courtesies, which belong to the diplomatic service, the successor of Mr. Motley at Vienna, and therefore familiar with his official record, not self-made, which too commonly means half-made, but with careful training added to the instincts to which he had a right by inheritance, he could not allow the memory of such a scholar, of such a high-minded lover of his country, of so true a gentleman as Mr. Motley, to remain without challenge under the stigma of official condemnation. I must refer to Mr. Jay's Memorial tribute as printed in the newspapers of the day, and to his "Appeal" published in the International Review, for his convincing presentation of the case, and content myself with a condensed statement of the general and special causes of complaint against Mr. Motley, and the explanations which suggest themselves, as abundantly competent to show the insufficiency of the reasons alleged by the Government as an excuse for the manner in which he was treated.

The grounds of complaint against Mr. Motley are to be looked for:

1. In the letter of Mr. Fish to Mr. Moran, of December 30, 1870.

Sect. XXI. 1869.

Examination of the ground of complaint against Mr. Motley.

2. In Mr. Bancroft Davis's letter to the New York Herald of January 4, 1878, entitled, "Mr. Sumner, the Alabama Claims and their Settlement."

3. The reported conversations of General Grant.

4. The reported conversations of Mr. Fish.

In considering Mr. Fish's letter, we must first notice its animus. The manner in which Dickens's two old women are brought in is not only indecorous, but it shows a state of feeling from which nothing but harsh interpretation of every questionable expression of Mr. Motley's was to be expected.

Interview with Lord Clarendon.

There is not the least need of maintaining the perfect fitness and rhetorical felicity of every phrase and every word used by him in his interview with Lord Clarendon. It is not to be expected that a minister, when about to hold a conversation with a representative of the government to which he is accredited, will commit his instructions to memory and recite them, like a school-boy "speaking his piece." He will give them more or less in his own language, amplifying, it may be, explaining, illustrating, at any rate paraphrasing in some degree, but endeavoring to convey an idea of their essential meaning. In fact, as any one can see, a *conversation* between two persons must necessarily imply a certain amount of extemporization on the part of both. I do not believe any long and important conference

Conversation implies extemporization.

was ever had between two able men without each of them feeling that he had not spoken exactly in all respects as he would if he could say all over again.

Doubtless, therefore, Mr. Motley's report of his conversation shows that some of his expressions might have been improved, and others might as well have been omitted. A man does not change his temperament on taking office. General Jackson still swore "by the Eternal," and his illustrious military successor of a more recent period seems, by his own showing, to have been liable to sudden impulses of excitement. It might be said of Motley, as it was said of Shakespeare by Ben Jonson, "aliquando sufflaminandus erat." Yet not too much must be made of this concession. Only a determination to make out a case could, as it seems to me, have framed such an indictment as that which the Secretary constructed by stringing together a slender list of pretended peccadillos. One instance will show the extreme slightness which characterizes many of the grounds of inculpation: —

Slightness of the grounds of inculpation.

The instructions say, "The government, in rejecting the recent convention, abandons neither its own claims nor those of its citizens," etc.

Mr. Motley said, in the course of his conversation, "At present, the United States Government, while withdrawing neither its national claims nor the

Sect. XXI.
1869–1870.

claims of its individual citizens against the British government," etc.

Mr. Fish says, "The determination of this government not to abandon its claims nor those of its citizens, was stated parenthetically, and in such a subordinate way as not necessarily to attract the attention of Lord Clarendon."

Captious criticism.

What reported conversation can stand a captious criticism like this? Are there not two versions of the ten commandments which were given out in the thunder and smoke of Sinai, and would the Secretary hold that this would have been a sufficient reason to recall Moses from his "Divine Legation" at the court of the Almighty?

There are certain expressions which, as Mr. Fish shows them *apart from their connection*, do very certainly seem in bad taste, if not actually indiscreet and unjustifiable. Let me give an example: ". . . . instead of expressing the hope entertained by this government that there would be an early, satisfactory, and friendly settlement of the questions at issue, he volunteered the unnecessary, and, from the manner in which it was thrust in, the highly objectionable statement that 'the United States Government had no insidious purposes,'" etc.

This sounds very badly as Mr. Fish puts it; let us see how it stands in its proper connection: —

"He [Lord Clarendon] added with some feeling, that in his opinion it would be highly objectionable that the question should be hung up on a peg, to be taken down at some convenient moment for us, when it might be difficult for the British government to enter upon its solution, and when they might go into the debate at a disadvantage. These were, as nearly as I can remember, his words, and I replied very earnestly that I had already answered that question when I said that my instructions were to propose as brief a delay as would probably be requisite for the cooling of passions and for producing the calm necessary for discussing the defects of the old treaty and a basis for a new one. The United States Government had no insidious purposes," etc.

Lord Clarendon's insinuation.

Motley's reply.

Is it not evident that Lord Clarendon suggested the idea which Mr. Motley repelled as implying an insidious mode of action? Is it not just as clear that Mr. Fish's way of reproducing the expression without the insinuation which called it forth is a practical misstatement which does Mr. Motley great wrong?

Unfair treatment of his words.

One more example of the method of wringing a dry cloth for drops of evidence ought to be enough to show the whole spirit of the paper.

Mr. Fish, in his instructions. "It might, indeed, well have occurred in the event of the selection by lot of the arbitrator or umpire in different cases, in-

Verbal criticism and strained inferences.

volving, however, precisely the same principles, that different awards, resting upon antagonistic principles, might have been made."

Mr. Motley, in the conversation with Lord Clarendon. . . . . "I called his lordship's attention to your very judicious suggestion that the throwing of the dice for umpires might bring about opposite decisions in cases arising out of identical principles. He agreed entirely that no principle was established by the treaty, but that the throwing of dice or drawing of lots was not a new invention on that occasion, but a not uncommon method in arbitrations. I only expressed the opinion that such an aleatory process seemed an unworthy method in arbitrations," etc.

Mr. Fish, in his letter to Mr. Moran. "That he had in his mind at that interview something else than his letter of instructions from this Department would appear to be evident, when he says that 'he called his lordship's attention to your [my] very judicious suggestion that the throwing of dice for umpire might bring about opposite decisions.' The instructions which Mr. Motley received from me contained no suggestion about 'throwing of dice.' That idea is embraced in the suggestive words 'aleatory process' (adopted by Mr. Motley), but previously applied in a speech made in the Senate on the question of ratifying the treaty."

Charles Sumner's Speech on the Johnson-Clarendon Treaty, April 13, 1869. . . . . "In the event of failure to agree, the arbitrator is determined 'by lot' out of two persons named by each side. Even if this aleatory proceeding were a proper device in the umpirage of private claims, it is strongly inconsistent with the solemnity which belongs to the present question."

It is "suggestive" that the critical Secretary, so keen in detecting conversational inaccuracies, having but two words to quote from a printed document, got one of them wrong. But this trivial comment must not lead the careful reader to neglect to note how much is made of what is really nothing at all. The word *aleatory*, whether used in its original and limited sense, or in its derived extension as a technical term of the civil law, was appropriate and convenient; one especially likely to be remembered by any person who had read Mr. Sumner's speech, — and everybody *had* read it, — the Secretary himself doubtless got the suggestion of determining the question "by lot" from it. What more natural than that it should be used again when the subject of appealing to chance came up in conversation? It "was an excellent good word before it was ill-sorted," and we were fortunate in having a minister who was scholar enough to know what it meant. The language

Aleatory.

Sect. XXI. 1869-1870.

Word-torturing as "showing animus."

used by Mr. Motley conveyed the idea of his instructions plainly enough, and threw in a compliment to their author which should have saved this passage at least from the wringing process. — The example just given is, like the concession of belligerency to the insurgents by Great Britain, chiefly important as "showing animus."

It is hardly necessary to bring forward other instances of virtual misrepresentation. If Mr. Motley could have talked his conversation over again, he would very probably have changed some expressions. But he felt bound to repeat the interview exactly as it occurred, with all the errors to which its extemporaneous character exposed it. When a case was to be made out against him, the Secretary wrote, December 30, 1870: —

A conversation disapproved.

"Well might he say, as he did in a subsequent despatch on the 15th of July, 1869, that he had gone beyond the strict letter of his instructions. He might have added, in direct opposition to their temper and spirit."

Of the same report the Secretary had said, June 28, 1869: —

The same conversation approved.

"Your general presentation and treatment of the several subjects discussed in that interview meet the approval of this Department." This general approval is qualified by mild criticism of a single statement as not having been conveyed in "precise conformity" to the President's view. The minister was told he might be well content to rest the question on the very forcible presentation he had made of the American side of the question, and that if there were expressions used stronger than were required by his instructions they were in the right direction. The mere fact that a minute of this conversation was confidentially submitted to Lord Clarendon in order that *our own Government* might have his authority for the accuracy of the record, which was intended exclusively for its own use, and that this circumstance was overlooked and not reported to the government until some weeks afterward, are the additional charges against Mr. Motley. The submission of the despatch containing an account of the interview, the Secretary says, is not inconsistent with diplomatic usage, but it is inconsistent with the duty of a minister not to inform his government of that submission. "Mr. Motley submitted the draft of his No. 8 to Lord Clarendon, and failed to communicate that fact to his government." — He did inform Mr. Fish, at any rate, on the 30th of July, and alleged "inadvertence" as the reason for his omission to do it before.

Submission of the minutes to Lord Clarendon.

This not inconsistent with diplomatic usage.

Inasmuch as submitting the despatch was not inconsistent with diplomatic usage, nothing seems left to find fault with but the not very long delay

Sect. XXI. 1869-1870.

in mentioning the fact, or in his making the note "private and confidential," as is so frequently done in diplomatic correspondence.

Such were the grounds of complaint. On the strength of the conversation which had met with the general approval of the government, tempered by certain qualifications, and of the omission to report *immediately* to the government the fact of its verification by Lord Clarendon, the Secretary rests the case against Mr. Motley. On these grounds it was that, according to him, the President withdrew all right to discuss the Alabama question from the minister whose dismissal was now only a question of time. — But other evidence comes in here.

The Alabama question.

Mr. Motley says, "It was, as I supposed, understood before my departure for England, although not publicly announced, that the so-called Alabama negotiations, whenever renewed, should be conducted at Washington, in case of the consent of the British Government."

Why the discussion was withdrawn from London.

Mr. Sumner says, in his "Explanation in Reply to an Assault," "the Secretary in a letter to me at Boston, dated at Washington, October 9, 1869, informs me that the discussion of the question was withdrawn from London '*because* (the italics are the Secretary's) we think that when renewed it can be carried on here with a better prospect of settlement, than where the late attempt at a convention which resulted so disastrously and was conducted so strangely was had'; and what the Secretary thus wrote he repeated in conversation when we met, carefully making the transfer to Washington depend upon our advantage here, from the presence of the Senate, — thus showing that the pretext put forth to wound Mr. Motley was an afterthought."

The despatch of September 25, 1869.

Again we may fairly ask how the government came to send a despatch like that of September 25, 1869, in which the views and expressions for which Mr. Motley's conversation had been criticised were so nearly reproduced, and with such emphasis that Mr. Motley says, in a letter to me, dated April 8, 1871, "It not only covers all the ground which I ever took, but goes far beyond it. No one has ever used stronger language to the British Government than is contained in that despatch. . . . . It is very able and well worth your reading. Lord Clarendon called it to me 'Sumner's speech over again.' It was thought by the English cabinet to have 'out-Sumnered Sumner,' and now our Government, thinking that every one in the United States had forgotten the despatch, makes believe that I was removed because my sayings and doings in England were too much influenced by Sumner!" Mr. Motley goes on to speak of the report that an offer of his place

It "out-Sumnered Sumner."

SECT. XXI. 1869-1870.

in England was made to Sumner "to get him out of the way of San Domingo." The facts concerning this offer are now sufficiently known to the public.

Here I must dismiss Mr. Fish's letter to Mr. Moran, having, as I trust, sufficiently shown the spirit in which it was written and the strained interpretations and manifest overstatements by which it attempts to make out its case against Mr. Motley. I will not parade the two old women, whose untimely and unseemly introduction into the dress-circle of diplomacy was hardly to have been expected of the high official whose name is at the bottom of this paper. They prove nothing, they disprove nothing, they illustrate nothing — except that a statesman may forget himself. Neither will I do more than barely allude to the unfortunate reference to the death of Lord Clarendon as connected with Mr. Motley's removal, so placidly disposed of by a sentence or two in the London Times of January 24, 1871. I think we may consider ourselves ready for the next witness.

Mr. Bancroft Davis's letter.

Mr. J. C. Bancroft Davis, Assistant Secretary of State under President Grant and Secretary Fish, wrote a letter to the New York Herald, under the date of January 4, 1878, since reprinted as a pamphlet and entitled "Mr. Sumner, the Alabama Claims and their Settlement." Mr. Sumner was

Mr. Davis's letter.

never successfully attacked when living, — except with a bludgeon, — and his friends have more than sufficiently vindicated him since his death. But Mr. Motley comes in for his share of animadversion in Mr. Davis's letter. He has nothing of importance to add to Mr. Fish's criticisms on the interview with Lord Clarendon. Only he brings out the head and front of Mr. Motley's offending by italicizing three very brief passages from his conversation at this interview; not discreetly, as it seems to me, for they will not bear the strain that is put upon them. These are the passages:—

He criticises three passages.

1. "*but that such measures must always be taken with a full view of the grave responsibilities assumed.*"

2. "*and as being the fountain head of the disasters which had been caused to the American people.*"

3. "*as the fruits of the proclamation.*"

"*Responsibility.*"

1. It is true that nothing was said of *responsibility* in Mr. Motley's instructions. But the idea was necessarily involved in their statements. For if, as Mr. Motley's instructions say, the right of a Power "to define its own relations," etc., when a civil conflict has arisen in another State depends on its (the conflict's) having "attained a sufficient complexity, magnitude, and completeness," inasmuch as that Power has to judge whether it has or

Sect. XXI. 1869-1870.

Mr. Davis's letter.

has not fulfilled these conditions, and is of course liable to judge wrong, every such act of judgment must be attended with grave responsibilities. The instructions say that "the necessity and propriety of the original concession of belligerency by Great Britain at the time it was made have been contested and are not admitted." It follows beyond dispute that Great Britain may in this particular case have incurred grave responsibilities; in fact, the whole negotiations implied as much. Perhaps Mr. Motley need not have used the word "responsibilities." But considering that the Government itself said in despatch No. 70, September 25, 1869, "The President does not deny, on the contrary he maintains, that every sovereign power decides for itself on its *responsibility* whether or not it will, at a given time, accord the status of belligerency," etc., it was hardly worth while to use italics about Mr. Motley's employment of the same language as constituting a grave cause of offence.

"Responsibility."

"Fountain head of disasters."

2. Mr. Motley's expression "as being *the fountain head of the disasters*," is a conversational paraphrase of the words of his instructions, "as it shows the beginning and the animus of that course of conduct which resulted so disastrously" which is not "in precise conformity" with his instructions, but is just such a variation as is to be expected when one is talking with another and using the words that

Mr. Davis's letter.

suggest themselves at the moment, just as the familiar expression "hung up on a peg" probably suggested itself to Lord Clarendon.

"*Fruits of the proclamation.*"

3. "the fruits of the proclamation" is so inconsiderable a variation on the text of the instructions "supplemented by acts causing direct damage" that the Secretary's hint about want of precise conformity seems hardly to have been called for.

It is important to notice this point in the instructions: With other Powers Mr. Motley was to take the position that the "recognition of the insurgents' state of war" was made "*no* ground of complaint"; with Great Britain that the cause of grievance was "*not so much*" placed upon the issuance of this recognition as upon her conduct under, and subsequent to, such recognition.

There is no need of maintaining the exact fitness of every expression used by Mr. Motley. But any candid person who will carefully read the government's despatch No. 70, dated September 25, 1869, will see that a government holding such language could find nothing in Mr. Motley's expressions in a conversation held at his first official interview to visit with official capital punishment more than a year afterwards. If Mr. Motley had, as it was pretended, followed Sumner, Mr. Fish had "out-Sumnered" the Senator himself.

Mr. Davis's pamphlet would hardly be complete

SECT. XXI. 1869-1870.

without a mysterious letter from an unnamed writer, whether a faithless friend, a disguised enemy, a secret emissary, or an injudicious alarmist, we have no means of judging for ourselves. The minister appears to have been watched by somebody in London, as he was in Vienna. This somebody wrote a private letter in which he expressed "fear and regret that Mr. Motley's bearing in his social intercourse was throwing obstacles in the way of a future settlement." The charge as mentioned in Mr. Davis's letter is hardly entitled to our attention. Mr. Sumner considered it the work of an enemy, and the recollection of the M'Crackin letter might well have made the government cautious of listening to complaints of such a character. This Somebody may have been one whom we should call Nobody. We cannot help remembering how well *Outis* served *Odusseus* of old, when he was puzzled to extricate himself from an embarrassing position. *Stat nominis umbra* is a poor showing for authority to support an attack on a public servant exposed to every form of open and insidious abuse from those who are prejudiced against his person or his birthplace, who are jealous of his success, envious of his position, hostile to his politics, dwarfed by his reputation, or hate him by the divine right of idiosyncrasy, always liable, too, to questioning comment from well-mean-

Somebody's private letter.

Its questionable value.

ing friends who happen to be suspicious or sensitive in their political or social relations.

Reputed sayings of General Grant and Mr. Fish.

The reported sayings of General Grant and of Mr. Fish to the correspondents who talked with them may be taken for what they are worth. They sound naturally enough to have come from the speakers who are said to have uttered them. I quote the most important part of the Edinburgh letter, September 11, 1877, to the New York Herald. These are the words attributed to General Grant.

General Grant's alleged explanation.

"Mr. Motley was certainly a very able, very honest gentleman, fit to hold any official position. But he knew long before he went out that he would have to go. When I was making these appointments, Mr. Sumner came to me and asked me to appoint Mr. Motley as minister to the court of St. James. I told him I would, and did. Soon after Mr. Sumner made that violent speech about the Alabama claims, and the British government was greatly offended. Mr. Sumner was at the time chairman of the Committee on Foreign Affairs. Mr. Motley had to be instructed. The instructions were prepared very carefully, and after Governor Fish and I had gone over them for the last time I wrote an addendum charging him that above all things he should handle the subject of the Alabama claims with the greatest delicacy. Mr. Motley, instead of obeying his explicit instructions,

SECT. XXI. 1869-1870.

General Grant's alleged explanation.

deliberately fell in line with Sumner and thus added insult to the previous injury. As soon as I heard of it I went over to the State Department and told Governor Fish to dismiss Motley at once. I was very angry indeed, and I have been sorry many a time since that I did not stick to my first determination. Mr. Fish advised delay because of Sumner's position in the Senate and attitude on the treaty question. We did not want to stir him up just then. We despatched a note of severe censure to Motley at once, and ordered him to abstain from any further connection with that question. We thereupon commenced negotiations with the British minister at Washington, and the result was the joint high commission and the Geneva award. I supposed Mr. Motley would be manly enough to resign after that snub, but he kept on till he was removed. Mr. Sumner promised me that he would vote for the treaty. But when it was before the Senate he did all he could to beat it."

General Grant talked again at Cairo, in Egypt.

Another alleged conversation with General Grant.

"Grant then referred to the statement published at an interview with him in Scotland, and said the publication had some omissions and errors. He had no ill-will towards Mr. Motley, who, like other estimable men, made mistakes, and Motley made a mistake which made him an improper person to hold office under me."

General Grant's alleged conversation.

"It is proper to say of me that I killed Motley, or that I made war upon Sumner for not supporting the annexation of San Domingo. But if I dare to answer that I removed Motley from the highest considerations of duty as an executive; if I presume to say that he made a mistake in his office which made him no longer useful to the country; if Fish has the temerity to hint that Sumner's temper was so unfortunate that business relations with him became impossible, we are slandering the dead."

Political incompatibilities.

"Nothing but Mortimer." Those who knew both men, — the Ex-President and the late Senator, — would agree, I do not doubt, that they would not be the most promising pair of human beings to make harmonious members of a political happy family. "*Cedant arma togæ*," the life-long sentiment of Sumner, in conflict with "Stand fast and stand sure," the well-known device of the clan of Grant, reminds one of the problem of an irresistible force in collision with an insuperable resistance. But the President says, — or is reported as saying, —"I may be blamed for my opposition to Mr. Sumner's tactics, but I was not guided so much by reason of his personal hatred of myself, as I was by a desire to protect our national interests in diplomatic affairs."

SECT. XXI. 1869-1870.

The useless controversy (Mr. Davis).

"It would be useless," says Mr. Davis in his letter to the Herald, "to enter into a controversy whether the President may or may not have been influenced in the final determination of the moment for requesting Motley's resignation by the feeling caused by Sumner's personal hostility and abuse of himself." Unfortunately, this controversy *had been* entered into, and the idleness of suggesting any relation of cause and effect between Mr. Motley's dismissal and the irritation produced in the President's mind by the rejection of the San Domingo treaty — which rejection was mainly due to Motley's friend Sumner's opposition — strongly insisted upon in a letter signed by the Secretary of State. *Too* strongly, for here it was that he failed to remember what was due to his office, to himself, and to the gentleman of whom he was writing; if indeed it was the Secretary's own hand which held the pen, and not another's.

Entered into by Mr. Fish.

We might as well leave out the wrath of Achilles from the Iliad, as the anger of the President with Sumner from the story of Motley's dismissal. The sad recital must always begin with **Μῆνιν ἄειδε.** He was, he is reported as saying, "very angry indeed" with Motley because he had *fallen in line* with Sumner. He couples them together in his conversation as closely as Chang and Eng were coupled. The death of Lord Clarendon would have covered

Μῆνιν ἄειδε.

The death of Lord Clarendon.

up the coincidence between the rejection of the San Domingo treaty and Mr. Motley's dismissal very neatly, but for the inexorable facts about its date, as revealed by the London Times. It betrays itself as an afterthought, and its failure as a defence reminds us too nearly of the trial in which Mr. Webster said suicide is confession.

An afterthought betrays itself.

It is not strange that the spurs of the man who had so lately got out of the saddle should catch in the scholastic robe of the man on the floor of the Senate. But we should not have looked for any such antagonism between the Secretary of State and the Envoy to Great Britain. On the contrary, they must have had many sympathies, and it must have cost the Secretary pain, as he said it did, to be forced to communicate with Mr. Moran instead of with Mr. Motley.

Mr. Fish's explanation of Mr. Motley's removal.

He too was inquired of by one of the emissaries of the American Unholy Inquisition. His evidence is thus reported: —

"The reason for Mr. Motley's removal was found in considerations of state. He misrepresented the government on the Alabama question, especially in the two speeches made by him before his arrival at his post."

Speeches at Liverpool.

These must be the two speeches made to the American and the Liverpool chambers of commerce. If there is anything in these short addresses beyond

SECT. XXI. 1869-1870.

Speeches at Liverpool.

those civil generalities which the occasion called out, I have failed to find it. If it was in these that the reason of Mr. Motley's removal was to be looked for, it is singular that they are not mentioned in the Secretary's letter to Mr. Moran, or by Mr. Davis in his letter to the New York Herald. They must have been as unsuccessful as myself in the search after anything in these speeches which could be construed into misinterpretation of the Government on the Alabama question.

"Considerations of state."

We may much more readily accept "considerations of state" as a reason for Mr. Motley's removal. *Considerations of state* have never yet failed the axe or the bowstring when a reason for the use of those convenient implements was wanted, and they are quite equal to every emergency which can arise in a republican autocracy. But for the very reason that a minister is absolutely in the power of his government, the manner in which that power is used is always open to the scrutiny, and, if it has been misused, to the condemnation, of a tribunal higher than itself; a court that never goes out of office, and which no personal feelings, no lapse of time, can silence.

The ostensible grounds on which Mr. Motley was recalled are plainly insufficient to account for the action of the Government. If it was in great measure a manifestation of personal feeling on the part of the high officials by whom and through whom the act was accomplished, it was a wrong which can never be repaired and never sufficiently regretted.

Stung by the slanderous report of an anonymous eavesdropper to whom the government of the day was not ashamed to listen, he had quitted Vienna, too hastily, it may be, but wounded, indignant, feeling that he had been unworthily treated. The sudden recall from London, on no pretext whatever but an obsolete and overstated incident which had ceased to have any importance, was under these circumstances a deadly blow. It fell upon "the new-healed wound of malice," and though he would not own it, and bore up against it, it was a shock from which he never fully recovered.

Effect of his recall upon Mr. Motley.

"I hope I am one of those," he writes to me from the Hague, in 1872, "who 'fortune's buffets and rewards can take with equal thanks.' I am quite aware that I have had far more than I deserve of political honors, and they might have had my post as a voluntary gift on my part had they remembered that I was an honorable man, and not treated me as a detected criminal deserves to be dealt with."

Mr. Sumner naturally felt very deeply what he considered the great wrong done to his friend. He says:—

Mr. Sumner's feeling on the subject.

"How little Mr. Motley merited anything but

SECT. XXI. 1869-1870.

Mr. Sumner's vindication of Mr. Motley.

respect and courtesy from the Secretary is attested by all who know his eminent position in London, and the service he rendered to his country. Already the London press, usually slow to praise Americans when strenuous for their country, has furnished its voluntary testimony. The Daily News of August 16, 1870, spoke of the insulted minister in these terms:—

Testimony of the London press.

"'We are violating no confidence in saying that all the hopes of Mr. Motley's official residence in England have been amply fulfilled, and that the announcement of his unexpected and unexplained recall was received with extreme astonishment and unfeigned regret. The vacancy he leaves cannot possibly be filled by a minister more sensitive to the honor of his government, more attentive to the interests of his country, and more capable of uniting the most vigorous performance of his public duties with the high-bred courtesy and conciliatory tact and temper that make those duties easy and successful. Mr. Motley's successor will find his mission wonderfully facilitated by the firmness and discretion that have presided over the conduct of American affairs in this country during too brief a term, too suddenly and unaccountably concluded.'"

No man can escape being found fault with when it is necessary to make out a case against him. A diplomatist is watched by the sharpest eyes and commented on by the most merciless tongues. The best and wisest has his defects, and sometimes they would seem to be very grave ones if brought up against him in the form of accusation. Take these two portraits, for instance, as drawn by John Quincy Adams. The first is that of Stratford Canning, afterwards Lord Stratford de Redcliffe:—

All men have their defects.

"He is to depart to-morrow. I shall probably see him no more. He is a proud, high-tempered Englishman, of good but not extraordinary parts; stubborn and punctilious, with a disposition to be overbearing, which I have often been compelled to check in its own way. He is, of all the foreign ministers with whom I have had occasion to treat, the man who has most severely tried my temper. Yet he has been long in the diplomatic career, and treated with governments of the most opposite characters. He has, however, a great respect for his word, and there is nothing false about him. This is an excellent quality for a negotiator. Mr. Canning is a man of forms, studious of courtesy, and tenacious of private morals. As a diplomatic man, his great want is suppleness, and his great virtue is sincerity."

Two characters, drawn by John Quincy Adams.

Stratford Canning.

The second portrait is that of the French minister, Hyde de Neuville:—

"No foreign minister who ever resided here has been so universally esteemed and beloved, nor have

Hyde de Neuville.

I ever been in political relations with any foreign statesman of whose moral qualities I have formed so good an opinion, with the exception of Count Romanzoff. He has not sufficient command of his temper, is quick, irritable, sometimes punctilious, occasionally indiscreet in his discourse, and tainted with Royalist and Bourbon prejudices. But he has strong sentiments of honor, justice, truth, and even liberty. His flurries of temper pass off as quickly as they rise. He is neither profound nor sublime nor brilliant; but a man of strong and good feelings, with the experience of many vicissitudes of fortune, a good but common understanding, and good intentions biassed by party feelings, occasional interests, and personal affections."

It means very little to say that a man has some human imperfections, or that a public servant might have done some things better. But when a questionable cause is to be justified the victim's excellences are looked at with the eyes of Brobdingnag and his failings with those of Liliput.

Recall of a foreign minister an exercise of despotic power.

The recall of a foreign minister for alleged misconduct in office is a kind of capital punishment. It is the nearest approach to the Sultan's bowstring which is permitted to the chief magistrate of our Republic. A general can do nothing under martial law more peremptory than a President can do with regard to the public functionary whom he has appointed with the advice and consent of the Senate, but whom he can officially degrade and disgrace at his own pleasure for insufficient cause or for none at all. Like the centurion of Scripture, he says Go, and he goeth. The Nation's Representative is less secure in his tenure of office than his own servant, to whom he must give warning of his impending dismissal.

> "A breath *unmakes him* as a breath has made."

Responsibility in proportion to power.

The chief magistrate's responsibility to duty, to the fellow-citizen at his mercy, to his countrymen, to mankind, is in proportion to his power. His prime minister, the agent of his edicts, should feel bound to withstand him if he seeks to gratify a personal feeling under the plea of public policy, unless the minister, like the slaves of the harem, is to find his qualification for office in leaving his manhood behind him.

The two successive administrations, which treated Mr. Motley in a manner unworthy of their position and cruel, if not fatal to him, have been heard, directly or through their advocates. I have attempted to show that the defence set up for their action is anything but satisfactory. A later generation will sit in judgment upon the evidence more calmly than our own. It is not for a friend, like the writer, to anticipate its decision, but unless the reasons alleged to justify his treatment, and which have so much the air of afterthoughts, shall seem stronger to that future tribunal than they do to him, the verdict will be that Mr. Motley was twice sacrificed to personal feelings which should never have been cherished by the heads of the government, and should never have been countenanced by their chief advisers.

XXII.

Life of John of Barneveld. — Criticisms. — Groen van Prinsterer. (1874.)

SECT. XXII. 1874.

Life of John of Barneveld.

THE full title of Mr. Motley's next and last work is "The Life and Death of John of Barneveld, Advocate of Holland; with a view of the primary causes and movements of the Thirty Years' War."

In point of fact this work is a history rather than a biography. It is an interlude, a pause between the acts which were to fill out the complete plan of the "Eighty Years' Tragedy," and of which the last act, the Thirty Years' War, remains unwritten. The Life of Barneveld was received as a fitting and worthy continuation of the series of intellectual labor in which he was engaged. I will quote but two general expressions of approval from the two best known British critical Reviews. In connection with his previous works, it forms, says the London Quarterly, "a fine and continuous story, of which the writer and the nation celebrated by him have equal reason to be proud; a narrative which will remain a prominent ornament of American genius, while it has permanently enriched Eng-

Criticisms. The London Quarterly.

Sect. XXII. 1874.

lish literature on this as well as on the other side of the Atlantic."

The Edinburgh Review.

The Edinburgh Review speaks no less warmly: "We can hardly give too much appreciation to that subtile alchemy of the brain which has enabled him to produce out of dull, crabbed, and often illegible state papers, the vivid, graphic, and sparkling narrative which he has given to the world."

M. Groen van Prinsterer.

In a literary point of view, M. Groen van Prinsterer, whose elaborate work has been already referred to, speaks of it as perhaps the most classical of Motley's productions, but it is upon this work that the force of his own and other Dutch criticisms has been chiefly expended.

Key to this biography.

The key to this biographical history or historical biography may be found in a few sentences from its opening chapter.

"There have been few men at any period whose lives have been more closely identical than his [Barneveld's] with a national history. There have been few great men in any history whose names have become less familiar to the world, and lived less in the mouths of posterity. Yet there can be no doubt that if William the Silent was the founder of the independence of the United Provinces, Barneveld was the founder of the Commonwealth itself. . . . .

"Had that country of which he was so long the

John of Barneveld.

first citizen maintained until our own day the same proportional position among the empires of Christendom as it held in the seventeenth century, the name of John of Barneveld would have perhaps been as familiar to all men as it is at this moment to nearly every inhabitant of the Netherlands. Even now political passion is almost as ready to flame forth, either in ardent affection or enthusiastic hatred, as if two centuries and a half had not elapsed since his death. His name is so typical of a party, a polity, and a faith, so indelibly associated with a great historical cataclysm as to render it difficult even for the grave, the conscientious, the learned, the patriotic of his own compatriots to speak of him with absolute impartiality.

Difficulty of impartiality.

"A foreigner who loves and admires all that is great and noble in the history of that famous republic, and can have no hereditary bias as to its ecclesiastical or political theories, may at least attempt the task with comparative coldness, although conscious of inability to do thorough justice to a most complex subject."

Mr. Motley a partisan of religious liberty and progress.

With all Mr. Motley's efforts to be impartial, to which even his sternest critics bear witness, he could not help becoming a partisan of the cause which for him was that of religious liberty and progress, as against the accepted formula of an old

SECT. XXII. 1874.

John of Barneveld.

ecclesiastical organization. For the quarrel which came near being a civil war, which convulsed the state, and cost Barneveld his head, had its origin in a difference on certain points, and more especially on a single point, of religious doctrine.

As a great river may be traced back until its fountain-head is found in a thread of water streaming from a cleft in the rocks, so a great national movement may sometimes be followed until its starting-point is found in the cell of a monk or the studies of a pair of wrangling professors.

Old controversies renewed.

The religious quarrel of the Dutchmen in the seventeenth century reminds us in some points of the strife between two parties in our own New England, sometimes arraying the "church" on one side against the "parish," or the general body of worshippers, on the other. The portraits of Gomarus, the great orthodox champion, and Arminius, the head and front of the "liberal theology" of his day, as given in the little old quarto of Meursius, recall two ministerial types of countenance familiar to those who remember the earlier years of our century.

Remonstrants and Contra-Remonstrants.

Under the name of "Remonstrants" and "Contra-Remonstrants,"—Arminians and old-fashioned Calvinists, as we should say,—the adherents of the two Leyden Professors disputed the right to the possession of the churches, and the claim to be

Life of John of Barneveld.

considered as representing the national religion. Of the seven United Provinces two, Holland and Utrecht, were prevailingly Arminian, and the other five Calvinistic. Barneveld, who, under the title of Advocate, represented the Province of Holland, the most important of them all, claimed for each Province a right to determine its own State religion. Maurice the Stadholder, son of William the Silent, the military chief of the Republic, claimed the right for the States-General. *Cujus regio ejus religio* was then the accepted public doctrine of Protestant nations. Thus the Provincial and the General governments were brought into conflict by their creeds, and the question whether the Republic was a Confederation or a Nation, the same question which has been practically raised, and for the time at least settled, in our own Republic, was in some way to be decided. After various disturbances and acts of violence by both parties, Maurice, representing the States-General, pronounced for the Calvinists or Contra-Remonstrants, and took possession of one of the great Churches, as an assertion of his authority. Barneveld, representing the Arminian, or Remonstrant Provinces, levied a body of mercenary soldiers in several of the cities. These were disbanded by Maurice, and afterwards by an act of the States-General. Barneveld was apprehended, imprisoned,

Conflict of authority.

John of Barneveld.

and executed, after an examination which was in no proper sense a trial. Grotius, who was on the Arminian side and involved in the inculpated proceedings, was also arrested and imprisoned. His escape, by a stratagem successfully repeated by a slave in our own times, may challenge comparison for its romantic interest with any chapter of fiction. How his wife packed him into the chest supposed to contain the folios of the great oriental scholar Erpenius, how the soldiers wondered at its weight, and questioned whether it did not hold an Arminian, how the servant-maid, Elsje van Houwening, quickwitted as Morgiana of the "Forty Thieves," parried their questions and convoyed her master safely to the friendly place of refuge, — all this must be read in the vivid narrative of the author.

Grotius.

The questions involved were political, local, personal, and above all religious. Here is the picture which Motley draws of the religious quarrel as it divided the people: —

The religious quarrel.

"In burghers' mansions, peasants' cottages, mechanics' back-parlors, on board herring-smacks, canal-boats, and East Indiamen; in shops, counting-rooms, farm-yards, guard-rooms, alehouses; on the exchange, in the tennis-court, on the mall; at banquets, at burials, christenings, or bridals; wherever and whenever human creatures met each other, there was ever to be found the fierce

John of Barneveld.

wrangle of Remonstrant and Contra-Remonstrant, the hissing of red-hot theological rhetoric, the pelting of hostile texts. The blacksmith's iron cooled on the anvil, the tinker dropped a kettle half mended, the broker left a bargain unclinched, the Scheveningen fisherman in his wooden shoes forgot the cracks in his pinkie, while each paused to hold high converse with friend or foe on fate, free-will, or absolute foreknowledge; losing himself in wandering mazes whence there was no issue. Province against province, city against city, family against family; it was one vast scene of bickering, denunciation, heart-burnings, mutual excommunication and hatred."

Grounds of the religious quarrel.

The religious grounds of the quarrel which set these seventeenth-century Dutchmen to cutting each other's throats were to be looked for in the "Five Points" of the Arminians as arrayed against the "Seven Points" of the Gomarites, or Contra-Remonstrants. The most important of the differences which were to be settled by fratricide seem to have been these: —

The Five Points.

According to the Five Points, "God has from eternity resolved to choose to eternal life those who through his grace believe in Jesus Christ," etc. According to the Seven Points, "God in his election has not looked at the belief and the repentance of the elect," etc. According to the Five Points, all

Sect. XXII. 1874.

John of Barneveld.

The Seven Saints.

good deeds must be ascribed to God's grace in Christ, but it does not work irresistibly. The language of the Seven Points implies that the elect cannot resist God's eternal and unchangeable design to give them faith and steadfastness, and that they can never wholly and for always lose the true faith. The language of the Five Points is unsettled as to the last proposition, but it was afterwards maintained by the Remonstrant party that a true believer could, through his own fault, fall away from God and lose faith.

Connection between religion and politics.

It must be remembered that these religious questions had an immediate connection with politics. Independently of the conflict of jurisdiction, in which they involved the parties to the two different creeds, it was believed or pretended that the new doctrines of the Remonstrants led towards Romanism, and were allied with designs which threatened the independence of the country. "There are two factions in the land," said Maurice, "that of Orange and that of Spain, and the two chiefs of the Spanish faction are those political and priestly Arminians, Uytenbogaert and Oldenbarneveld."

The heads of the two religious and political parties were in such hereditary, long-continued, and intimate relations up to the time when one signed the other's death-warrant, that it was impossible to write the life of one without also writing that of the other. For his biographer John of Barneveld is the true patriot, the martyr, whose cause was that of religious and political freedom. For him Maurice is the ambitious soldier who hated his political rival, and never rested until this rival was brought to the scaffold.

John of Barneveld.

The questions which agitated men's minds two centuries and a half ago are not dead yet in the country where they produced such estrangement, violence, and wrong. No stranger could take them up without encountering hostile criticism from one party or the other. It may be and has been conceded that Mr. Motley writes as a partisan, — a partisan of freedom in politics and religion, as he understands freedom. This secures him the antagonism of one class of critics. But these critics are themselves partisans, and themselves open to the cross-fire of their antagonists. M. Groen van Prinsterer, "the learned and distinguished" Editor of the Archives et Correspondance of the Orange and Nassau family, published a considerable volume, before referred to, in which many of Motley's views are strongly controverted. But he himself is far from being in accord with "that eminent scholar," M. Bakhuyzen van den Brink, whose name, he says, is celebrated enough to need no comment, or with M. Fruin, of whose impartiality and erudition he himself speaks in the strongest terms. The

M. Groen van Prinsterer's work.

SECT. XXII. 1874.

John of Barneveld.

ground upon which he is attacked is thus stated in his own words: —

"People have often pretended to find in my writings the deplorable influence of an extreme Calvinism. The Puritans of the seventeenth century are my fellow-religionists. I am a *sectarian* and not an *historian*."

It is plain enough to any impartial reader that there are at least plausible grounds for this accusation against Mr. Motley's critic. And on a careful examination of the formidable volume, it becomes obvious that Mr. Motley has presented a view of the events and the personages of the stormy epoch with which he is dealing, which leaves a battle-ground yet to be fought over by those who come after him. The dispute is not and cannot be settled.

The end of all religious discussion has come when one of the parties claims that it is thinking or acting under immediate Divine guidance. "It is God's affair, and his honor is touched," says William Lewis to Prince Maurice. Mr. Motley's critic is not less confident in claiming the Almighty as on the side of his own views. Let him state his own ground of departure:—

M. Groen van Prinsterer's ground of departure.

"To show the difference, let me rather say the contrast, between the point of view of Mr. Motley and my own, between the *Unitarian* and the *Evan-*

gelical belief. "I am *issue of* CALVIN, child of the *Awakening* (reveil). Faithful to the device of the Reformers: *Justification* by *faith alone, and the Word of God endures eternally.* I consider history from the point of view of *Merle d'Aubigné,* Chalmers, Guizot. I desire to be *disciple* and *witness* of our Lord and Saviour, Jesus Christ."

John of Barneveld.

The Calvinist.

He is therefore of necessity antagonistic to a writer whom he describes in such words as these: —

"Mr. Motley is *liberal* and *rationalist.*

"He becomes, in attacking the principle of the Reformation, the passionate opponent of the Puritans and of Maurice, the ardent apologist of Barnevelt and the *Arminians.*

"It is understood, and he makes no mystery of it, that he inclines towards the vague and undecided doctrine of the Unitarians."

The Unitarian, accord. to his opponent.

What M. Groen's idea of Unitarians is may be gathered from the statement about them which he gets from a letter of De Tocqueville.

"They are pure deists; they talk about the Bible, because they do not wish to shock too severely public opinion, which is prevailingly *Christian.* They have a service on Sundays, I have been there. At it they read verses from Dryden or other English poets on the existence of God and the immortality of the soul. They deliver a discourse on some point of morality, and all is said."

Sect. XXII. 1874.

John of Barneveld.

In point of fact the wave of protest which stormed the dikes of Dutch orthodoxy in the seventeenth century stole gently through the bars of New England puritanism in the eighteenth.

Protests against Calvinism.

"Though the large number," says Mr. Bancroft, "still acknowledged the fixedness of the divine decrees, and the resistless certainty from all eternity of election and of reprobation, there were not wanting, even among the clergy, some who had modified the sternness of the ancient doctrine by making the self-direction of the active powers of man with freedom of inquiry and private judgment the central idea of a protest against Calvinism."

Perplexities of Protestantism.

Protestantism, cut loose from an infallible church, and drifting with currents it cannot resist, wakes up once or oftener in every century, to find itself in a new locality. Then it rubs its eyes and wonders whether it has found its harbor or only lost its anchor. There is no end to its disputes, for it has nothing but a fallible vote as authority for its oracles, and these appeal only to fallible interpreters.

It is as hard to contend in argument against "the oligarchy of heaven," as Motley calls the Calvinistic party, as it was formerly to strive with them in arms.

To this "aristocracy of God's elect" belonged the party which framed the declaration of the Synod

John of Barneveld.

of Dort; the party which under the forms of justice shed the blood of the great statesman who had served his country so long and so well. To this chosen body belonged the late venerable and truly excellent as well as learned M. Groen van Prinsterer, and he exercised the usual right of examining in the light of his privileged position the views of a "liberal" and "rationalist" writer who goes to meeting on Sunday to hear verses from Dryden. This does not diminish his claim for a fair reading of the "intimate correspondence," which he considers Mr. Motley has not duly taken into account, and of the other letters to be found printed in his somewhat disjointed and fragmentary volume.

The "intimate correspondence."

This "intimate correspondence" shows Maurice the Stadholder indifferent and lax in internal administration and as being constantly advised and urged by his relative Count William of Nassau. This need of constant urging extends to religious as well as other matters, and is inconsistent with M. Groen van Prinsterer's assertion that the question was for Maurice above all religious, and for Barneveld above all political. Whether its negative evidence can be considered as neutralizing that which is adduced by Mr. Motley to show the Stadholder's hatred of the Advocate may be left to the reader who has just risen from the account

SECT. XXII. 1874.

John of Barneveld.

of the mock trial and the swift execution of the great and venerable statesman. The formal entry on the Record upon the day of his "judicial murder" is singularly solemn and impressive: —

Record of Barneveld's execution.

"Monday, 13th May, 1619. To-day was executed with the sword here in the Hague, on a scaffold thereto erected in the Binnenhof before the steps of the great hall, Mr. John of Barneveld, in his life Knight, Lord of Berkel, Rodenrys, etc., Advocate of Holland and West Friesland, for reasons expressed in the sentence and otherwise, with confiscation of his property, after he had served the state thirty-three years two months and five days, since 8th March, 1586; a man of great activity, business, memory and wisdom — yea, extraordinary in every respect. He that stands let him see that he does not fall."

Maurice gave an account of the execution of Barneveld to Count William Lewis on the same day in a note "painfully brief and dry."

Authors are autobiographers.

Most authors write their own biography consciously or unconsciously. We have seen Mr. Motley portraying much of himself, his course of life and his future, as he would have had it, in his first story. In this, his last work, it is impossible not to read much of his own external and internal personal history told under other names and with different

John of Barneveld.

accessories. The parallelism often accidentally or intentionally passes into divergence. He would not have had it too close if he could, but there are various passages in which it is plain enough that he is telling his own story.

Self-portraiture.

Mr. Motley was a diplomatist, and he writes of other diplomatists, and one in particular, with most significant detail. It need not be supposed that he intends the "arch intriguer" Aerssens to stand for himself, or that he would have endured being thought to identify himself with the man of whose "almost devilish acts" he speaks so freely. But the sagacious reader — and he need not be very sharp-sighted — will very certainly see something more than a mere historical significance in some of the passages which I shall cite for him to reflect upon. Mr. Motley's standard of an ambassador's accomplishments may be judged from the following passage.

Accomplishments of Dutch Ministers.

"That those ministers [those of the Republic] were second to the representatives of no other European state in capacity and accomplishment was a fact well known to all who had dealings with them, for the states required in their diplomatic representatives knowledge of history and international law, modern languages, and the classics, as well as familiarity with political customs and social courtesies; the breeding of gentlemen, in short; and the accomplishments of scholars."

John of Barneveld.

The story of the troubles of Aerssens, the Ambassador of the United Provinces at Paris, must be given at some length, and will repay careful reading.

Francis Aerssens.

"Francis Aerssens . . . . continued to be the Dutch ambassador after the murder of Henry IV. . . . . He was beyond doubt one of the ablest diplomatists in Europe. Versed in many languages, a classical student, familiar with history and international law, a man of the world and familiar with its usages, accustomed to associate with dignity and tact on friendliest terms with sovereigns, eminent statesmen, and men of letters; endowed with a facile tongue, a fluent pen, and an eye and ear of singular acuteness and delicacy; distinguished for unflagging industry and singular aptitude for secret and intricate affairs; — he had by the exercise of these various qualities during a period of nearly twenty years at the court of Henry the Great been able to render inestimable services to the Republic which he represented.

"He had enjoyed the intimacy and even the confidence of Henry IV., so far as any man could be said to possess that monarch's confidence, and his friendly relations and familiar access to the king gave him political advantages superior to those of any of his colleagues at the same court.

"Acting entirely and faithfully according to the

Sect. XXII. 1874.

John of Barneveld.

instructions of the Advocate of Holland, he always gratefully and copiously acknowledged the privilege of being guided and sustained in the difficult paths he had to traverse by so powerful and active an intellect. I have seldom alluded in terms to the instructions and despatches of the chief, but every position, negotiation, and opinion of the envoy — and the reader has seen many of them — is pervaded by their spirit. . . . .

"It had become a question whether he was to remain at his post or return. It was doubtful whether he wished to be relieved of his embassy or not. The States of Holland voted 'to leave it to his candid opinion if in his free conscience he thinks he can serve the public any longer. If yes, he may keep his office one year more. If no, he may take leave and come home.'

Aerssens courteously treated.

"Surely the States, under the guidance of the Advocate, had thus acted with consummate courtesy towards a diplomatist whose position, from no apparent fault of his own, but by the force of circumstances — and rather to his credit than otherwise — was gravely compromised."

The Queen, Mary de' Medici, had a talk with him, got angry, " became very red in the face," and wanted to be rid of him.

"Nor was the Envoy at first desirous of remaining. . . . . Nevertheless, he yielded reluctantly to

Sect. XXII. 1874.

John of Barneveld.

Barneveld's request that he should, for the time at least, remain at his post. Later on, as the intrigues against him began to unfold themselves, and his faithful services were made use of at home to blacken his character and procure his removal, he refused to resign, as to do so would be to play into the hands of his enemies, and, by inference at least, to accuse himself of infidelity to his trust." . . . .

Aerssens intrigued against.

"It is no wonder that the Ambassador was galled to the quick by the outrage which those concerned in the government were seeking to put upon him. How could an honest man fail to be overwhelmed with rage and anguish at being dishonored before the world by his masters for scrupulously doing his duty, and for maintaining the rights and dignity of his own country? He knew that the charges were but pretexts, that the motives of his enemies were as base as the intrigues themselves, but he also knew that the world usually sides with the government against the individual, and that a man's reputation is rarely strong enough to maintain itself unsullied in a foreign land when his own government stretches forth its hand, not to shield, but to stab him. . . . .

Attempt to drive him from his post

"'I know,' he said, 'that this plot has been woven partly in Holland and partly here by good correspondence, in order to drive me from my post with disreputation. . . . .

John of Barneveld.

"'But as I have discovered this accurately, I have resolved to offer to my masters the continuance of my very humble service for such time and under such conditions as they may think good to prescribe. I prefer forcing my natural and private inclinations to giving an opportunity for the ministers of this kingdom to discredit us, and to my enemies to succeed in injuring me, and by fraud and malice to force me from my post. . . . . I am truly sorry, being ready to retire, wishing to have an honorable testimony in recompense of my labors, that one is in such hurry to take advantage of my fall. . . . . What envoy will ever dare to speak with vigor if he is not sustained by the government at home? . . . . My enemies have misrepresented my actions, and my language as passionate, exaggerated, mischievous, but I have no passion except for the service of my superiors. . . . .'

Aerssens intends to remain.

"Barneveld, from well-considered motives of public policy, was favoring his honorable recall. But he allowed a decorous interval of more than three years to elapse in which to terminate his affairs, and to take a deliberate departure from that French embassy to which the Advocate had originally promoted him, and in which there had been so many years of mutual benefit and confidence between the two statesmen. He used no underhand means. He did not abuse the power of the States-General

Respectfully treated by his government.

SECT. XXII. 1874.

which he wielded to cast him suddenly and brutally from the distinguished post which he occupied, and so to attempt to dishonor him before the world. Nothing could be more respectful and conciliatory than the attitude of the government from first to last towards this distinguished functionary. The Republic respected itself too much to deal with honorable agents whose services it felt obliged to dispense with as with vulgar malefactors who had been detected in crime. . . . .

An implied contrast.

"This work aims at being a political study. I would attempt to exemplify the influence of individual humors and passions — some of them among the highest and others certainly the basest that agitate humanity — upon the march of great events, upon general historical results at certain epochs, and upon the destiny of eminent personages."

Influence of individual humors and passions.

Here are two suggestive portraits: —

"The Advocate, while acting only in the name of a slender confederacy, was in truth, so long as he held his place, the prime minister of European Protestantism. There was none other to rival him, few to comprehend him, fewer still to sustain him. As Prince Maurice was at that time the great soldier of Protestantism, without clearly scanning the grandeur of the field in which he was a chief actor, or foreseeing the vastness of its future, so the Advocate was its statesman and its prophet. Could the two have worked together as harmoniously as they had done at an earlier day, it would have been a blessing for the common weal of Europe. But, alas! the evil genius of jealousy, which so often forbids cordial relations between soldier and statesman, already stood shrouded in the distance, darkly menacing the strenuous patriot, who was wearing his life out in exertions for what he deemed the true cause of progress and humanity. . . . .

The soldier and the statesman.

"All history shows that the brilliant soldier of a republic is apt to have the advantage, in a struggle for popular affection and popular applause, over the statesman, however consummate. . . . . The great battles and sieges of the Prince had been on a world's theatre, had enchained the attention of Christendom, and on their issue had frequently depended, or seemed to depend, the very existence of the nation. The labors of the statesman, on the contrary, had been comparatively secret. His noble orations and arguments had been spoken with closed doors to assemblies of colleagues — rather envoys than senators —. . . . while his vast labors in directing both the internal administration and especially the foreign affairs of the commonwealth had been by their very nature as secret as they were perpetual and enormous."

The reader of the life of Barneveld must judge

SECT. XXII. 1874.

John of Barneveld.

for himself whether in these and similar passages the historian was thinking solely of Maurice, the great military leader, of Barneveld, the great statesman, and of Aerssens, the recalled ambassador. He will certainly find that there were "burning questions" for ministers to handle then as now, and recognize in "that visible atmosphere of power the poison of which it is so difficult to resist" a respiratory medium as well known to the nineteenth as to the seventeenth century.

XXIII.

Death of Mrs. Motley. — Last Visit to America. — Illness and Death. — Lady Harcourt's Communication. (*1874-1877.*)

SECT. XXIII. 1874-1877.

Death of Mrs. Motley.

ON the last day of 1874 the beloved wife, whose health had for some years been failing, was taken from him by death. She had been the pride of his happier years, the stay and solace of those which had so tried his sensitive spirit. The blow found him already weakened by mental suffering and bodily infirmity, and he never recovered from it.

Mr. Motley visits America.

Mr. Motley's last visit to America was in the summer and autumn of 1875. During several weeks which he passed at Nahant, a seaside resort near Boston, I saw him almost daily. He walked feebly and with some little difficulty, and complained of a feeling of great weight in the right arm, which made writing laborious. His handwriting had not betrayed any very obvious change, so far as I had noticed in his letters. His features and speech were without any paralytic character. His mind was clear except when, as on one or two occasions, he complained of some confused feeling, and

SECT. XXIII 1874-1877.

walked a few minutes in the open air to compose himself. His thoughts were always tending to revert to the almost worshipped companion from whom death had parted him a few months before. Yet he could often be led away to other topics, and in talking of them could be betrayed into momentary cheerfulness of manner. His long-enduring and all-pervading grief was not more a tribute to the virtues and graces of her whom he mourned than an evidence of the deeply affectionate nature which in other relations endeared him to so many whose friendship was a title to love and honor.

I have now the privilege of once more recurring to the narrative of Mr. Motley's daughter, Lady Harcourt.

His daughter Lady Harcourt's account.

"The harassing work and mental distress of this time [after the recall from England] acting on an acutely nervous organization, began the process of undermining his constitution, of which we were so soon to see the results. It was not the least courageous act of his life, that, smarting under a fresh wound, tired and unhappy, he set his face immediately towards the accomplishment of fresh literary labor. After my sister's marriage in January he went to the Hague to begin his researches in the archives for John of Barnevelt. The Queen of the Netherlands had made ready a house for us,

Lady Harcourt's account.

and personally superintended every preparation for his reception. We remained there until the spring, and then removed to a house more immediately in the town, a charming old-fashioned mansion, once lived in by John de Witt, where he had a large library and every domestic comfort during the year of his sojourn. The incessant literary labor in an enervating climate with enfeebled health may have prepared the way for the first break in his constitution, which was to show itself soon after. There were many compensations in the life about him. He enjoyed the privilege of constant companionship with one of the warmest hearts and finest intellects which I have ever known in a woman — the *âme d'élite* which has passed beyond this earth. The gracious sentiment with which the Queen sought to express her sense of what Holland owed him would have been deeply felt even had her personal friendship been less dear to us all. From the King, the society of the Hague, and the diplomatic circle we had many marks of kindness. Once or twice I made short journeys with him for change of air to Amsterdam, to look for the portraits of John of Barneveld and his wife; to Bohemia, where, with the lingering hope of occupying himself with the Thirty Years' War, he looked carefully at the scene of Wallenstein's death near Prague, and later to Varzin in Pomerania for a

The Queen of the Netherlands.

Journeys.

SECT. XXIII. 1874.

week with Prince Bismarck, after the great events of the Franco-German war. In the autumn of 1872 we moved to England, partly because it was evident that his health and my mother's required a change; partly for private reasons to be near my sister and her children. The day after our arrival at Bournemouth occurred the rupture of a vessel on the lungs, without any apparently sufficient cause. He recovered enough to revise and complete his manuscript, and we thought him better, when at the end of July, in London, he was struck down by the first attack of the head, which robbed him of all after power of work, although the intellect remained untouched. Sir William Gull sent him to Cannes for the winter, where he was seized with a violent internal inflammation, in which I suppose there was again the indication of the lesion of blood-vessels. I am nearing the shadow now — the time of which I can hardly bear to write. You know the terrible sorrow which crushed him on the last day of 1874, — the grief which broke his heart and from which he never rallied. From that day it seems to me that his life may be summed up in the two words, — patient waiting. Never for one hour did her spirit leave him, and he strove to follow its leading for the short and evil days left and the hope of the life beyond. I think I have never watched quietly and reverently the traces of

Lady Harcourt's account.

Illness.

one personal character remaining so strongly impressed on another nature. With her self-depreciation and unselfishness she would have been the last to believe how much of him was in her very existence; nor could we have realized it until the parting came. Henceforward, with the mind still there, but with the machinery necessary to set it in motion disturbed and shattered, he could but try to create small occupations with which to fill the hours of a life which was only valued for his children's sake. Kind and loving friends in England and America soothed the passage, and our gratitude for so many gracious acts is deep and true. His love for children, always a strong feeling, was gratified by the constant presence of my sister's babies, the eldest a little girl who bore my mother's name, and had been her idol, being the companion of many hours and his best comforter. At the end the blow came swiftly and suddenly, as he would have wished it. It was a terrible shock to us who had vainly hoped to keep him a few years longer, but at least he was spared what he had dreaded with a great dread, a gradual failure of mental or bodily power. The mind was never clouded, the affections never weakened, and after a few hours of unconscious physical struggle he lay at rest, his face beautiful and calm, without a trace of suffering or illness. Once or twice he said, 'It has

SECT. XXIII. 1874-1877.

The last hour.

come, it has come,' and there were a few broken words before consciousness fled, but there was little time for messages or leave-taking. By a strange coincidence his life ended near the town of Dorchester, in the mother country, as if the last hour brought with it a reminiscence of his birthplace, and of his own dearly loved mother. By his own wish only the dates of his birth and death appear upon his gravestone, with the text chosen by himself, 'In God is light, and in him is no darkness at all.'"

XXIV.

Conclusion.—His Character.—His Labors.—His Reward.

In closing this restricted and imperfect record of a life which merits, and in due time will, I trust, receive an ampler tribute, I cannot refrain from adding a few thoughts which naturally suggest themselves, and some of which may seem quite unnecessary to the reader who has followed the story of the historian and diplomatist's brilliant and eventful career.

Sect. XXIV. 1814–1877.

His endowments.

Mr. Motley came of a parentage which promised the gifts of mind and body very generally to be accounted for, in a measure at least, wherever we find them, by the blood of one or both of the parents. They gave him special attractions and laid him open to not a few temptations. Too many young men born to shine in social life, to sparkle, it may be, in conversation, perhaps in the lighter walks of literature, become agreeable idlers, self-indulgent, frivolous, incapable of large designs or sustained effort, lose every aspiration and forget every ideal. Our gilded youth want such examples as this of Motley, not a solitary, but a conspicuous one, to teach them how much better is the restlessness of a noble ambition than the narcotized stupor of club-life or the vapid amusement of a dressed-up intercourse which too often requires a questionable flavor of forbidden license to render it endurable to persons of vivacious character and temperament.

His temperament.

It would seem difficult for a man so flattered from his earliest days to be modest in his self-estimate; but Motley was never satisfied with himself. He was impulsive, and was occasionally, I have heard it said, over excited, when his prejudices were roughly handled. In all that related to the questions involved in our civil war, he was, no doubt, very sensitive. He had heard so much that exasperated him in the foreign society which he had expected to be in full sympathy with the cause of liberty as against slavery, that he might be excused if he showed impatience when he met with similar sentiments among his own countrymen. He felt that he had been cruelly treated by his own government, and no one who conceives himself to have been wronged and insulted must be expected to reason in naked syllogisms on the propriety of the liberties which have been taken with his name and standing. But with all his quickness of feeling his manners were easy and courteous, simply because his nature was warm and kindly, and with all his natural fastidiousness there was nothing of the coxcomb about him.

Sect. XXIV. 1814-1877.

His gifts not a recommendation to all.

He must have had enemies, as all men of striking individuality are sure to have; his presence cast more uncouth patriots into the shade; his learning was a reproach to the ignorant, his fame was too bright a distinction; his high-bred air and refinement, which he could not help, would hardly commend him to the average citizen in an order of things in which mediocrity is at a premium, and the natural nobility of presence, which rarely comes without family antecedents to account for it, is not always agreeable to the many whose two ideals are the man on horseback and the man in his shirt-sleeves. It may well be questioned whether Washington, with his grand manner, would be nearly as popular with what are called "the masses" as Lincoln, with his homely ways and broad stories. The experiment of universal suffrage must render the waters of political and social life more or less turbid even if they remain innoxious. The Cloaca Maxima can hardly mingle its contents with the stream of the Aqua Claudia, without taking something from its crystal clearness. We need not go so far as one of our well-known politicians has recently gone in saying that no great man can reach the highest position in our government, but

SECT. XXIV. 1814–1877.

we can safely say that, apart from military fame, the loftiest and purest and finest personal qualities are not those which can be most depended upon at the ballot-box. Strange stories are told of avowed opposition to Mr. Motley on the ground of the most trivial differences in point of taste in personal matters, — so told that it is hard to disbelieve them, and they show that the caprices which we might have thought belonged exclusively to absolute rulers among their mistresses or their minions may be felt in the councils of a great people which calls itself self-governing. It is perfectly true that Mr. Motley did not illustrate the popular type of politician. He was too high-minded, too scholarly, too generously industrious, too polished, too much at home in the highest European circles, too much courted for his personal fascinations, too remote from the trading world of caucus managers. To degrade him, so far as official capital punishment could do it, was not merely to wrong one whom the nation should have delighted to honor as showing it to the world in the fairest flower of its young civilization, but it was an indignity to a representative of the highest scholarship of native growth, which every student in the land felt as a discouragement to all sound learning and noble ambition.

Disqualifying accomplishments.

If he was disappointed in his diplomatic career,

he had enough, and more than enough, to console him in his brilliant literary triumphs. He had earned them all by the most faithful and patient labor. If he had not the "frame of adamant" of the Swedish hero, he had his "soul of fire." No labors could tire him, no difficulties affright him. What most surprised those who knew him as a young man was, not his ambition, not his brilliancy, but his dogged, continuous capacity for work. We have seen with what astonishment the old Dutch scholar, Groen van Prinsterer, looked upon a man who had wrestled with authors like Bor and Van Meteren, who had grappled with the mightiest folios and toiled undiscouraged among half-illegible manuscript records. Having spared no pains in collecting his materials, he told his story, as we all know, with flowing ease and stirring vitality. His views may have been more or less partial; Philip the Second may have deserved the pitying benevolence of poor Maximilian; Maurice may have wept as sincerely over the errors of Arminius as any one of "the crocodile crew that believe in election"; Barneveld and Grotius may have been on the road to Rome; none of these things seem probable, but if they were all proved true in opposition to his views, we should still have the long roll of glowing tapestry he has woven for us, with all its life-like portraits, its almost moving

His untiring industry.

Life and coloring of his style.

Sect. XXIV. 1814-1877.

His fame.

pageants, its sieges where we can see the artillery flashing, its battle-fields with their smoke and fire, — pictures which cannot fade and which will preserve his name interwoven with their own enduring colors.

His treatment.

Republics are said to be ungrateful; it might be truer to say that they are forgetful. They forgive those who have wronged them as easily as they forget those who have done them good service. But History never forgets and never forgives. To her decision we may trust the question, whether the warm-hearted patriot who had stood up for his country nobly and manfully in the hour of trial,

His record.

the great scholar and writer who had reflected honor upon her throughout the world of letters, the high-minded public servant, whose shortcomings it taxed the ingenuity of experts to make conspicuous enough to be presentable, was treated as such a citizen should have been dealt with. His record is safe in

His memory.

her hands, and his memory will be precious always in the hearts of all who enjoyed his friendship.

APPENDIX.

A.

The Saturday Club.

[SEE PAGE 119.]

APPENDIX A.

The Saturday Club.

THIS Club, of which we were both members, and which is still flourishing, came into existence in a very quiet sort of way at about the same time as the Atlantic Monthly, and although entirely unconnected with that magazine, included as members some of its chief contributors. Of those who might have been met at some of the monthly gatherings in its earlier days I may mention Emerson, Hawthorne, Longfellow, Lowell, Motley, Whipple, Whittier; Professors Agassiz and Peirce; John S. Dwight; Governor Andrew, Richard H. Dana, Junior, Charles Sumner. It offered a wide gamut of intelligences, and the meetings were noteworthy occasions. If there was not a certain amount of "mutual admiration" among some of those I have mentioned it was a great pity, and implied a defect in the nature of

APPENDIX A.

The Satur-Club.

men who were otherwise largely endowed. The vitality of this club has depended in a great measure on its utter poverty in statutes and by-laws, its entire absence of formality, and its blessed freedom from speech-making.

That holy man, Richard Baxter, says in his Preface to "Alleine's Alarm": "I have done, when I have sought to remove a little scandal, which I foresaw, that I should myself write the Preface to his Life where himself and two of his friends make such a mention of my name, which I cannot own; which will seem a praising him for praising me. I confess it looketh ill-favoredly in me. But I had not the power of other men's writings, and durst not forbear that which was his due."

I do not know that I have any occasion for a similar apology in printing the following lines read at a meeting of members of the Saturday Club and other friends who came together to bid farewell to Motley before his return to Europe in 1857.

A PARTING HEALTH.

A parting health.

Yes, we knew we must lose him, — though friendship
may claim
To blend her green leaves with the laurels of fame,
Though fondly, at parting, we call him our own,
'T is the whisper of love when the bugle has blown.

A parting health.

As the rider that rests with the spur on his heel, —
As the guardsman that sleeps in his corselet of steel, —
As the archer that stands with his shaft on the string,
He stoops from his toil to the garland we bring.

What pictures yet slumber unborn in his loom
Till their warriors shall breathe and their beauties shall
bloom,
While the tapestry lengthens the life-glowing dyes
That caught from our sunsets the stain of their skies!

In the alcoves of death, in the charnels of time,
Where flit the dark spectres of passion and crime,
There are triumphs untold, there are martyrs unsung,
There are heroes yet silent to speak with his tongue!

Let us hear the proud story that time has bequeathed
From lips that are warm with the freedom they breathed!
Let him summon its tyrants, and tell us their doom,
Though he sweep the black past like Van Tromp with
his broom!

. . . . .

The dream flashes by, for the west-winds awake
On pampas, on prairie, o'er mountain and lake,
To bathe the swift bark, like a sea-girdled shrine
With incense they stole from the rose and the pine.

APPENDIX A.

A parting health.

So fill a bright cup with the sunlight that gushed
When the dead summer's jewels were trampled and crushed;
THE TRUE KNIGHT OF LEARNING, — the world holds him dear, —
Love bless him, joy crown him, God speed his career!

Appendix B.

Habits and Methods of Study.

APPENDIX B.

Modes of life and habits of work.

MR. MOTLEY'S daughter, Lady Harcourt, has favored me with many interesting particulars which I could not have learned except from a member of his own family. Her description of his way of living and of working will be best given in her own words: —

"He generally rose early, the hour varying somewhat at different parts of his life, according to his work and health. Sometimes when much absorbed by literary labor he would rise before seven, often lighting his own fire, and with a cup of tea or coffee writing until the family breakfast hour, after which his work was immediately resumed, and he usually sat over his writing-table until late in the afternoon, when he would take a short walk. His dinner hour was late, and he rarely worked at night. During the early years of his literary studies he led a life of great retirement. Later, after the publication of the Dutch Republic and during the years of official place, he was much in society in England, Austria, and Holland. He enjoyed social life, and

APPENDIX B.

Modes of life and habits of work.

particularly dining out, keenly, but was very moderate and simple in all his personal habits, and for many years before his death had entirely given up smoking. His work, when not in his own library, was in the Archives of the Netherlands, Brussels, Paris, the English State Paper Office, and the British Museum, where he made his own researches, patiently and laboriously consulting original manuscripts and reading masses of correspondence, from which he afterwards sometimes caused copies to be made, and where he worked for many consecutive hours a day. After his material had been thus painfully and toilfully amassed, the writing of his own story was always done at home, and his mind, having digested the necessary matter, always poured itself forth in writing so copiously that his revision was chiefly devoted to reducing the over-abundance. He never shrank from any of the drudgery of preparation, but I think his own part of the work was sheer pleasure to him."

I should have mentioned that his residence in London while Minister was at the house No. 17 Arlington Street, belonging to Lord Yarborough.

Appendix C.

Sir William Gull's Account of his Illness.

APPENDIX C.

Sir William Gull's account of Mr. Motley's illness.

I HAVE availed myself of the permission implied in the subjoined letter of Sir William Gull to make large extracts from his account of Mr. Motley's condition while under his medical care. In his earlier years he had often complained to me of those "nervous feelings connected with the respiration" referred to by this very distinguished physician. I do not remember any other habitual trouble to which he was subject.

74 BROOK STREET, GROSVENOR SQUARE, W.
February 13, 1878.

MY DEAR SIR, — I send the notes of Mr. Motley's last illness, as I promised. They are too technical for general readers, but you will make such exception as you require. The medical details may interest your professional friends. Mr. Motley's case was a striking illustration that the renal disease of so-called Bright's disease may supervene as part

APPENDIX C.

Sir William Gull's account of Mr. Motley's illness.

and parcel of a larger and antecedent change in the blood-vessels in other parts than the kidney. . . .
I am, my dear sir,

Yours very truly,

WILLIAM W. GULL.

TO OLIVER WENDELL HOLMES, ESQ.

I first saw Mr. Motley, I believe, about the year 1870, on account of some nervous feelings connected with the respiration. At that time his general health was good, and all he complained of was occasionally a feeling of oppression about the chest. There were no physical signs of anything abnormal, and the symptoms quite passed away in the course of time, and with the use of simple antispasmodic remedies, such as camphor and the like. This was my first interview with Mr. Motley, and I was naturally glad to have the opportunity of making his acquaintance. I remember that in our conversation I jokingly said that my wife could hardly forgive him for not making her hero, Henri IV., a perfect character, and the earnestness with which he replied *au serieux,* "I assure you I have fairly recorded the facts." After this date I did not see Mr. Motley for some time. He had three slight attacks of hæmoptysis in the autumn of 1872, but no physical signs of change in the lung tissue re-

Sir William Gull's account of his illness.

sulted. So early as this I noticed that there were signs of commencing thickening in the heart, as shown by the degree and extent of its impulse. The condition of his health, though at that time not very obviously failing, a good deal arrested my attention, as I thought I could perceive in the occurrence of the hæmoptysis, and in the cardiac hypertrophy, the early beginnings of vascular degeneration.

In August, 1873, occurred the remarkable seizure, from the effects of which Mr. Motley never recovered. I did not see him in the attack, but was informed, as far as I can remember, that he was on a casual visit at a friend's house at luncheon (or it might have been dinner), when he suddenly became strangely excited, but not quite unconscious. . . . . I believed at the time, and do so still, that there was some capillary apoplexy of the convolutions. The attack was attended with some hemiplegic weakness on the right side, and altered sensation, and ever after there was a want of freedom and ease both in the gait and in the use of the arm of that side. To my inquiries from time to time how the arm was, the patient would always flex and extend it freely, but nearly always used the expression, "There is a bedevilment in it"; though the hand-writing was not much, if at all, altered.

APPENDIX C.

Sir William Gull's account of his illness.

In December, 1873, Mr. Motley went by my advice to Cannes. I wrote the following letter* at the time to my friend Dr. Frank, who was practising there: —

December 29, 1873.

His letter to Dr. Frank.

MY DEAR DR. FRANK, — My friend Mr. Motley, the historian and late American Minister, whose name and fame no doubt you know very well, has by my advice come to Cannes for the winter and spring, and I have promised him to give you some account of his case. To me it is one of special interest, and personally, as respects the subject of it, of painful interest. I have known Mr. Motley for some time, but he consulted me for the present condition about midsummer.

.... If I have formed a correct opinion of the pathology of the case, I believe the smaller vessels are degenerating in several parts of the *vascular area*, lung, brain, and kidneys. With this view I have suggested a change of climate, a nourishing diet, etc.; and it is to be hoped, and I trust expected, that by great attention to the conditions of hygiene, internal and external, the progress of degeneration may be retarded. I have no doubt you will find, as time goes on, increasing evidence of

* This letter, every word of which was of value to the practitioner who was to have charge of the patient, relates many of the facts given above, and I shall therefore only give extracts from it.

Sir William Gull's account of his illness.

renal change, but this is rather a coincidence and consequence than a cause, though no doubt when the renal change has reached a certain point, it becomes in its own way a factor of other lesions. I have troubled you at this length because my mind is much occupied with the pathology of these cases, and because no case can, on personal grounds, more strongly challenge our attention.

Yours very truly,

WILLIAM W. GULL.

During the spring of 1874, whilst at Cannes, Mr. Motley had a sharp attack of nephritis, attended with fever; but on returning to England in July there was no important change in the health. The weakness of the side continued, and the inability to undertake any mental work. The signs of cardiac hypertrophy were more distinct. In the beginning of the year 1875 I wrote as follows: —

February 20, 1875.

MY DEAR MR. MOTLEY, — . . . . The examination I have just made appears to indicate that the main conditions of your health are more stable than they were some months ago, and would therefore be so far in favor of your going to America in the summer, as we talked of. The ground of my doubt has lain in the possibility of such a trip further disor-

APPENDIX C.

Sir William Gull's account of his illness.

dering the circulation. Of this, I hope, there is now less risk.

On the 4th of June, 1875, I received the following letter.

Mr. Motley's letter to Sir William Gull

CALVERLY PARK HOTEL, TUNBRIDGE WELLS,
June 4, 1875.

MY DEAR SIR WILLIAM, — I have been absent from town for a long time, but am to be there on the 9th and 10th. Could I make an appointment with you for either of those days? I am anxious to have a full consultation with you before leaving for America. Our departure is fixed for the 19th of this month. I have not been worse than usual of late. I think myself, on the contrary, rather stronger, and it is almost impossible for me not to make my visit to America this summer, unless you should absolutely prohibit it. If neither of those days should suit you, could you kindly suggest another day? I hope, however, you can spare me half an hour on one of those days, as I like to get as much of this bracing air as I can. Will you kindly name the hour when I may call on you, and address me at this hotel. Excuse this slovenly note in pencil, but it fatigues my head and arm much more to sit at a writing-table with pen and ink.

Always most sincerely yours,
My dear Sir William.
J. L. MOTLEY.

Sir William Gull's account of his illness.

On Mr. Motley's return from America I saw him, and found him, I thought, rather better in general health than when he left England.

In December, 1875, Mr. Motley consulted me for trouble of vision in reading or walking, from sensations like those produced by flakes of falling snow coming between him and the objects he was looking at. Mr. Bowman, one of our most excellent oculists, was then consulted. Mr. Bowman wrote to me as follows: "Such symptoms as exist point rather to disturbed retinal function than to any brain-mischief. It is, however, quite likely that what you fear for the brain may have had its counterpart in the nerve-structures of the eye, and as he is short-sighted, this tendency may be further intensified."

Mr. Bowman suggested no more than such an arrangement of glasses as might put the eyes, when in use, under better optic conditions.

The year 1876 was passed over without any special change worth notice. The walking powers were much impeded by the want of control over the right leg. The mind was entirely clear, though Mr. Motley did not feel equal, and indeed had been advised not to apply himself to any literary work. Occasional conversations, when I had interviews with him on the subject of his health, proved that the attack which had weakened the move-

Sir William Gull's account of his illness.

ments of the right side had not impaired the mental power. The most noticeable change which had come over Mr. Motley since I first knew him was due to the death of Mrs. Motley in December, 1874. It had in fact not only profoundly depressed him, but, if I may so express it, had removed the centre of his thought to a new world. In long conversations with me of a speculative kind, after that painful event, it was plain how much his point of view of the whole course and relation of things had changed. His mind was the last to dogmatize on any subject. There was a candid and childlike desire to know, with an equal confession of the incapacity of the human intellect. I wish I could recall the actual expressions he used, but the sense was that which has been so well stated by Hooker in concluding an exhortation against the pride of the human intellect, where he remarks: —

His mental condition.

"Dangerous it were for the feeble brain of man to wade far into the doings of the Most High; whom although to know be life, and joy to make mention of His Name, yet our soundest knowledge is to know that we know Him, not indeed as He is, neither can know Him; and our safest eloquence concerning Him is our silence, when we confess without confession that His glory is inexplicable, His greatness above our capacity and reach. He is above and we upon earth;

therefore it behoveth our words to be wary and few."

Sir William Gull's account of his illness.

Mrs. Motley's illness was not a long one, and the nature of it was such that its course could with certainty be predicted. Mr. Motley and her children passed the remaining days of her life, extending over about a month, with her, in the mutual understanding that she was soon to part from them. The character of the illness, and the natural exhaustion of her strength by suffering, lessened the shock of her death, though not the loss, to those who survived her.

Mrs. Motley's illness and death.

The last time I saw Mr. Motley was, I believe, about two months before his death, March 28th, 1877. There was no great change in his health, but he complained of indescribable sensations in his nervous system, and felt as if losing the whole power of walking, but this was not obvious in his gait, although he walked shorter distances than before. I heard no more of him until I was suddenly summoned on the 29th of May into Devonshire to see him. The telegram I received was so urgent, that I suspected some rupture of a blood-vessel in the brain, and that I should hardly reach him alive; and this was the case. About two o'clock in the day he complained of a feeling of faintness, said he felt ill and should not recover; and in a few minutes was insensible with symptoms of ingravescent

Appendix C.

apoplexy. There was extensive hæmorrhage into the brain, as shown by post-mortem examination, the cerebral vessels being atheromatous. The fatal hæmorrhage had occurred into the lateral ventricles, from rupture of one of the middle cerebral arteries.

I am, my dear Sir,

Yours very truly,

WILLIAM W. GULL.

Appendix D.

Place of Burial.—Funeral Service.—Epitaphs.—Dean Stanley's Funeral Sermon.

APPENDIX D.

Funeral of Mr. Motley.

MR. MOTLEY was buried by the side of his wife in Kensal Green Cemetery, just outside of London. Services were held in the chapel at the cemetery.

The following account of the funeral is extracted from a letter of Mr. Smalley to the New York Tribune:—

Mr. Smalley's account.

"Mr. Motley was buried on Monday in Kensal Green Cemetery, Dean Stanley performing the service. The funeral was neither quite public nor quite private. It had been Dean Stanley's wish that it should take place in Westminster Abbey. He had proposed that the body, when brought from Dorsetshire, should lie over night in the Abbey; that a ceremony should be held there in the morning, and that the friends of the deceased should assemble at the Abbey and accompany the body thence to the cemetery. But some difficulties—I could not make out what—stood in the way of this arrangement. It is cause for regret that the kind purposes of the Dean could not be carried

APPENDIX D.

Funeral of Mr. Motley.

Mr. Smalley's account.

out. Mr. Motley's friends — and all Americans, because he was an American — would have liked that some of the last words said over him should have been said in the great church which has so peculiar an interest for Americans, — which Americans in general venerate as they venerate no cathedral and no other church. As it was not to be, we can only express our gratitude to Dean Stanley for his readiness to bring it about.

"The service at the Kensal Green Chapel was of course the burial service of the Church of England, of which Mr. Motley was a member. His three daughters, Lady Harcourt, Mrs. Sheridan, and Miss Motley, were present, and with Sir William Harcourt, Mr. Russell Sturgis, and Mr. Sheridan, followed the coffin from the chapel to the grave. Among others present were Mr. Bright, the Duke of Argyll, Mr. Froude, Lord Houghton, Mr. Thomas Hughes, the Minister of the Netherlands, the Minister of Belgium, the Hon. Lyulph Stanley, Mr. Lecky, Mr. Hoppin, Mr. Murray, Mr. Edward Dicey, and Mr. Conway."

The inscriptions on the gravestones are these: —

JOHN LOTHROP MOTLEY.

BORN AT DORCHESTER, MASS., APRIL 15, 1814.

DIED NEAR DORCHESTER, DORSET, MAY 29, 1877.

In God is light, and in him is no darkness at all.

MARY ELIZABETH, WIFE OF JOHN LOTHROP MOTLEY.

BORN APRIL 7, 1813.

DIED DECEMBER 31, 1874.

Truth shall make you free.

On the 3d of June Dean Stanley preached a sermon in Westminster Abbey, in which he referred with much feeling to the death of Mr. Motley. I give a few extracts from the manuscript notes sent me by Miss Motley.

Extract from Dean Stanley's sermon.

". . . . But there is a yet deeper key of harmony that has just been struck within the last week. The hand of death has removed from his dwelling-place amongst us one of the brightest lights of the Western hemisphere, — the high-spirited patriot, the faithful friend of England's best and purest spirits, the brilliant, the indefatigable historian who told as none before him had told the history of the rise and struggle of the Dutch Republic, almost a part of his own.

"We sometimes ask what room or place is left in the crowded temple of Europe's fame for one of the Western world to occupy. But a sufficient answer is given in the work which was reserved to be accomplished by him who has just departed. So long as the tale of the greatness of the house of Orange, of the siege of Leyden, of the tragedy of Barneveld, interests mankind, so long will Hol-

APPENDIX D.

Extract from Dean Stanley's sermon.

land be indissolubly connected with the name of Motley in that union of the ancient culture of Europe with the aspirations of America which was so remarkable in the ardent, laborious, soaring soul that has passed away. He loved that land of his with a passionate zeal, he loved the land of his adoption with a surpassing love. . . . . He loved the fatherland, the mother tongue of the literature which he had made his own. He loved the land which was the happy home of his children, and which contained the dearly cherished grave of her beside whom he will be laid to-morrow. Whenever any gifted spirit passes from our world to the other it brings both within our nearer view, — the world of this mortal life with its contentions and strifes, its joys and griefs, now to him closed forever, but amidst which he won his fame, and in which his name shall long endure, and the other world of our ideal vision, of our inexhaustible longings, of our blank misgivings, of our inextinguishable hopes, of our everlasting reunions, the eternal love in which live the spirits of the just made perfect, the heavenly Jerusalem, which being above is free, the city of which God himself is the light, and in whose light we shall see light."

Appendix E.

From the Proceedings of the Massachusetts Historical Society.

APPENDIX E.

Tributes of the Mass. Historical Society.

AT a meeting of the Massachusetts Historical Society, held on Thursday, the 14th of June, 1877, after the reading of the records of the preceding meeting, the President, the Hon. Robert C. Winthrop, spoke as follows : —

Hon. R. C. Winthrop's remarks.

" Our first thoughts to-day, gentlemen, are of those whom we may not again welcome to these halls. We shall be in no mood, certainly, for entering on other subjects this morning, until we have given some expression to our deep sense of the loss — the double loss — which our Society has sustained since our last monthly meeting." . . . . *

After a most interesting and cordial tribute to his friend, Mr. Quincy, Mr. Winthrop continued :—

" The death of our distinguished associate, Motley, can hardly have taken many of us by surprise. Sudden at the moment of its occurrence, we had

* Edmund Quincy died May 17. John Lothrop Motley died May 29.

APPENDIX E.

Mass. Hist. Society. Mr. Winthrop's remarks.

long been more or less prepared for it by his failing health. It must, indeed, have been quite too evident to those who had seen him, during the last two or three years, that his life-work was finished. I think he so regarded it himself.

"Hopes may have been occasionally revived in the hearts of his friends, and even in his own heart, that his long-cherished purpose of completing a History of the Thirty Years' War, as the grand consummation of his historical labors, — for which all his other volumes seemed to him to have been but the preludes and overtures, — might still be accomplished. But such hopes, faint and flickering from his first attack, had wellnigh died away. They were like Prescott's hopes of completing his Philip the Second, or like Macaulay's hopes of finishing his brilliant History of England.

"But great as may be the loss to literature of such a crowning work from Motley's pen, it was by no means necessary to the completeness of his own fame. His 'Rise of the Dutch Republic,' his 'History of the United Netherlands,' and his 'Life of John of Barneveld," had abundantly established his reputation, and given him a fixed place among the most eminent historians of our country and of our age.

"No American writer, certainly, has secured a wider recognition or a higher appreciation from the

Mass. Hist. Society. Mr. Winthrop's remarks.

scholars of the Old World. The Universities of England and the learned societies of Europe have bestowed upon him their largest honors. It happened to me to be in Paris when he was first chosen a corresponding member of the Institute, and when his claims were canvassed with the freedom and earnestness which peculiarly characterize such a candidacy in France. There was no mistaking the profound impression which his first work had made on the minds of such men as Guizot and Mignet. Within a year or two past a still higher honor has been awarded him from the same source. The journals not long ago announced his election as one of the six foreign associates of the French Academy of Moral and Political Sciences, — a distinction which Prescott would probably have attained had he lived a few years longer, until there was a vacancy, but which, as a matter of fact, I believe, Motley was the only American writer, except the late Edward Livingston, of Louisiana, who has actually enjoyed.

"Residing much abroad, for the purpose of pursuing his historical researches, he had become the associate and friend of the most eminent literary men in almost all parts of the world, and the singular charms of his conversation and manners had made him a favorite guest in the most refined and exalted circles.

APPENDIX E.

Mass. Hist. Society. Mr. Winthrop's remarks.

"Of his relations to political and public life, this is hardly the occasion or the moment for speaking in detail. Misconstructions and injustices are the proverbial lot of those who occupy eminent position. It was a duke of Vienna, if I remember rightly, whom Shakespeare, in his 'Measure for Measure,' introduces as exclaiming,—

> 'O place and greatness, millions of false eyes
> Are stuck upon thee! Volumes of report
> Run with these false and most contrarious quests
> Upon thy doings! Thousand 'scapes of wit
> Make thee the father of their idle dream,
> And rack thee in their fancies!'

"I forbear from all application of the lines. It is enough for me, certainly, to say here, to-day, that our country was proud to be represented at the courts of Vienna and London successively by a gentleman of so much culture and accomplishment as Mr. Motley, and that the circumstances of his recall were deeply regretted by us all.

"His fame, however, was quite beyond the reach of any such accidents, and could neither be enhanced or impaired by appointments or removals. As a powerful and brilliant historian we pay him our unanimous tribute of admiration and regret, and give him a place in our memories by the side of Prescott and Irving. I do not forget how many of us lament him, also, as a cherished friend.

Mass. Hist. Society. Mr. Winthrop's remarks.

"He died on the 29th ultimo, at the house of his daughter, Mrs. Sheridan, in Dorsetshire, England, and an impressive tribute to his memory was paid, in Westminster Abbey, on the following Sunday, by our Honorary Member, Dean Stanley. Such a tribute, from such lips, and with such surroundings, leaves nothing to be desired in the way of eulogy. He was buried in Kensal Green Cemetery, by the side of his beloved wife.

"One might well say of Motley precisely what he said of Prescott, in a letter from Rome to our associate, Mr. William Amory, immediately on hearing of Prescott's death: 'I feel inexpressibly disappointed — speaking now for an instant purely from a literary point of view — that the noble and crowning monument of his life, for which he had laid such massive foundations, and the structure of which had been carried forward in such a grand and masterly manner, must remain uncompleted, like the unfinished peristyle of some stately and beautiful temple on which the night of time has suddenly descended. But, still, the works which his great and untiring hand had already thoroughly finished will remain to attest his learning and genius, — a precious and perpetual possession for his country.'

"I am authorized by the Council to offer the following resolutions: —

. . . . . .

APPENDIX E.

Mass. Hist. Society.

Resolves offered.

"'*Resolved,* That by the death of the Hon. John Lothrop Motley this Society has lost one of its most distinguished members, and American literature one of its brightest ornaments; a son of Massachusetts, who, in illustrating so powerfully the annals of another land, has reflected the highest honor on his own, and whose fame as an historian will ever be cherished among the treasures of his native State.

"'*Resolved,* That the President be requested to nominate one of our associates to prepare a Memoir of Mr. Motley.'"

Mr. Amory's remarks.

William Amory, Esq., spoke as follows: —

"I thank you cordially, Mr. President, for affording to me at this time the opportunity of paying the tribute of a few remarks to the memory of one whom I had so long known, loved, and honored as Mr. Motley; and, though I may fail to do it in words suitable to the occasion, or satisfactory to myself, I am compelled by the promptings of my heart, not alone in silence to mingle my tears with those of the family and friends who mourn the loss of a father, brother, and friend, but to join also my voice with the voices of those who are gathered here to-day to deplore the loss and honor the memory of him who, as our associate, by his writings and character has contributed so largely to elevate

Mass. Hist. Society. Mr. Amory's remarks.

the reputation of this Society, to embellish the name of this community, and to reflect throughout the civilized world the lustre of his own name on the literature of his native country. Till about 1840 I personally knew little of Mr. Motley; but since then our intimacy has been unbroken and our intercourse uninterrupted, except by his absence in Europe. The lapse of almost forty years since I first saw him has scarcely effaced from the freshness of my memory my first impression of the transparent nature and striking idiosyncrasies of his remarkable character, which made it easy to imagine the past, and not difficult to divine the future of his brilliant career. The expressive beauty of his face, the manly elegance of his person, his winning ways, his sparkling wit, and the irresistible charm of his conversation, all gave even then assurance of distinction and promise of fame in his riper years. A few years later, at about thirty, not inclined to the practice of the law, which he had studied partly as an accomplishment, partly as a possible means of support, and partly as a preparation for any other pursuit he might embrace as more congenial to his temperament or taste, he determined upon a literary career, and, as his genius, attainments, studies, and tastes inclined him thereto, he, fortunately for himself and the world, adopted history as a specialty, and selected 'The

APPENDIX E.

Mass. Hist. Society. Mr. Amory's remarks.

Rise of the Dutch Republic' as the subject of his first historical work.

"His brilliant success a few years later, on the publication of that book, showed how wisely he had chosen for his own reputation, for the honor of the republic whose history he faithfully, picturesquely, and elegantly depicted, and for that of the republic at home, upon which he at once shed such glory as a writer. By this, his first history, published in London in 1856, he was raised by common consent at one bound to the front rank of illustrious historians in the English language, and by his subsequent works, though perhaps less attractive to the general reader, he has sustained the reputation he at that time acquired.

"With a few of his friends in this country, I was favored with the privilege of a perusal of those volumes before they were published in England; and, though already entertaining a high appreciation of his genius and powers, I was inexpressibly surprised at the eloquence of the style, the interest of the narrative, the variety, aptitude, and brilliancy of the illustrations, and the life-like fidelity of the portraits of the chief actors in that wonderful historical drama, but above all by the untiring industry and diligent research displayed throughout in procuring, preparing, and using so ably such copious materials from such various sources. Three

Mass. Hist. Society. Mr. Amory's remarks.

years after its publication, in 1859, Mr. Motley, on hearing of the death of W. H. Prescott, his friend and brother historian, wrote from Rome a long letter, containing a very interesting account of an interview he had sought with Mr. Prescott about twelve years before, in relation to the subject of the Rise of the Dutch Republic. That letter was read by Mr. Sears at a meeting of this Society, holden in April, 1859, and recorded in full on page 266 of the published 'Proceedings' of 1858–60. Though too long to be read here, it is so touching and beautiful a letter, and so creditable and honorable to both Mr. Motley and Mr. Prescott, that I have ventured to allude to it for the benefit of such members of this Society as have either forgotten or never seen it, and to whom at this moment it may have a peculiar interest, if they possess the volume of the 'Proceedings' referred to. The subject of the letter may be briefly stated thus: About 1846, Mr. Motley had collected materials and made preparations to write 'The Rise of the Dutch Republic,' ignorant of the fact that Mr. Prescott had still earlier also made still larger preparations to write the 'History of Philip II.' As, in writing upon subjects so closely identified in time and events, it was obvious that Mr. Motley must often traverse the same ground occupied by Mr. Prescott, he determined, when informed by a friend of Mr. Prescott's

APPENDIX E.

Mass. Hist. Society. Mr. Amory's remarks.

intention, to go to him and confer with him on the subject; and, if he should find that Mr. Prescott had a shadow of objection to his proceeding with his history, to abandon it at once, though already so enamored of the subject he had selected that it was to him, as he said, like surrendering his historical career. He did so, was most kindly received, and cordially encouraged to proceed with the work at once by Mr. Prescott, who, at the same time, generously volunteered to offer any aid in his power and the free use of his library.

"Such is the summary of the purpose and result of that interview; but to realize the sacrifice which the young aspirant to authorship was ready to make to a nice sense of honor and courtesy to the perhaps doubtful priority of the conventional claim of one with whom at that time he was only slightly acquainted, or to appreciate the genuine gratitude and pleasure inspired by the cordial aid and generous encouragement offered him by Mr. Prescott, it is necessary to read the letter itself.

"I have, Mr. President, perhaps dwelt too long on this subject; but the temptation to present in one picture, and to illustrate by one anecdote, the different, but equally beautiful, traits of character exhibited in the same story by the two most illustrious historians of this country must be my excuse.

"You may well be proud, sir, that during your

Mass. Hist. Society. Mr. Amory's remarks.

presidency of the Massachusetts Historical Society the names of Prescott and Motley, both your associates, have been enrolled by universal consent in the same rank with those of Hume, Gibbon, and Robertson, of the eighteenth century, and Hallam and Macaulay, of the nineteenth; and it is worth recording on the same page that these friends and brother historians of the same subject were natives of the same State, citizens of the same city, graduates of the same college, equally remarkable for their personal beauty and the charms of their manners, published their first histories at the same time of life, and died in precisely the same manner, at about the same age. With more time, it would be gratifying to compare and contrast those elements of moral, intellectual, and social character, which, though so different in each of these distinguished men, contributed so equally to the charms and celebrity of both in the world of letters and in the society of the world; but it is too late, and I am conscious that already I have encroached upon the ground of his literary friends, instead of confining myself to those social and domestic beauties of his character, so much richer in interest and materials, and upon which I am so much better authority. One of these attributes, and, as I think, the most prominent and characteristic of all, was the tender affectionateness of his nature, which,

Mass. Hist. Society. Mr. Amory's remarks.

within the small circle of his home and friends, was irresistibly winning, and which, though less known to the outside world, pervaded his whole being, and was often the hidden source of that magnetism and fascination which captivated all, and won for him hosts of friends and admirers wherever he was known.

"His ready and deep sympathy in the hour of sorrow or affliction, as indicated by the tones of his voice, the expression of his face, or the simple eloquence of his words, will be long remembered by many. Passing by that greatest and last domestic affliction, which made his home so desolate and his life so sad for the last two years, as too recent and sacred to be more than glanced at, I recall that agony of grief occasioned many years before by the sudden and shocking death of his nearest and dearest friend, Mr. Stackpole. Mr. Motley, for a while at that time a near neighbor of mine, spent every afternoon with me on my piazza at Longwood; and I shall never forget the touching words and manner in which he bewailed his loss in all the variety of thought and language which death and friendship could suggest, and with all the eloquence of an 'In Memoriam.' He could think and talk of nothing else. Subdued and softened by his sorrow, he seemed an altered man, and in the tenderness of his grief he was more like a mother weeping for

Mass. Hist. Society. Mr. Amory's remarks.

an only child than a strong man mourning the loss even of his dearest friend. How easy it would be, Mr. President, to select from a character so rich in its endless variety many other equally interesting peculiarities, and to illustrate them by similar reminiscences, no one can imagine without a familiar acquaintance with the incidents of his life, and a nice appreciation of those fine impulses of his nature which have shaped his career; and this can be fitly done only by the eloquent pen of a biographer who has known him from his youth.

"I have made no allusion to Mr. Motley's diplomatic career, which, but for circumstances beyond his control and not attributable to any fault of his, might have been as distinguished as his career as a writer, because I am sure that, to all who knew him, or the history of the termination of his missions to Vienna and London, any defence of *him certainly*, on either side of the water, would be entirely superfluous."

The President now called on Dr. Oliver Wendell Holmes, who said:—

Dr. Holmes's remarks.

"The thoughts which suggest themselves upon this occasion are such as belong to the personal memories of the dear friends whom we have lost, rather than to their literary labors, the just tribute to which must wait for a calmer hour than the

APPENDIX E.

Mass. Hist. Society. Dr. Holmes's remarks.

present, following so closely as it does on our bereavement.

"To those of us who remember Mr. Motley during his last visit to this country, his death, though it was a blow to many lingering hopes, was hardly a surprise. But if we go back a few more years, and recall him as he appeared at our meeting of November, 1868, he comes before us with the promise of a long afternoon and evening to a life which was still in the brightness of its intellectual meridian. It fell to him on that occasion to speak before us of his friend, the late Dean Milman, and I am sure that not one of those who listened to him can forget the effect his words and his presence produced upon all who were gathered around him.

"He stood before us, a scholar speaking of a man of letters, and his words had the fitness, the balance, the flow, which belong to an imperial master of language. He was speaking of one who was, as he said, 'his life long a conspicuous ornament of the most cultivated society of London and of England'; and here was in his own person and address that harmonious union of rare qualities which all the world over is the master-key that opens every door, the countersign that passes every sentinel, the unsealed letter of introduction to all the highest circles of the highest civilization. Scholars are frequently forgetful of the outward

Mass. Hist. Society. Dr. Holmes's remarks.

graces which commend the man of the world to social favor. Here was a scholar who, to say the least, had rivalled the most robust and patient of our workers in drudgery, who had ploughed through manuscripts without number, whose crabbed characters and uncouth phrases might well have tried Champollion's temper; yet here was a man of such natural graces and such distinguished bearing, that he seemed to belong rather to the gilded saloon than to the dusty library.

"Let me touch briefly upon a few periods in his life. I remember him as a handsome, spirited-looking boy at Harvard College, where, at the early age of thirteen, he joined the class two years after my own, graduating in 1831. He was probably the youngest student in college, said to be as bright as he looked, and with the reputation of a remarkable talent for learning languages. Two years make a wide gulf in college life, and my intercourse with him was less frequent than at a later period. I recollect him in those earlier days as vivacious, attractive, brilliant, with such a lustre of promise about him as belonged to hardly any other of my own date, and after it, in my four years' college experience, if I perhaps except William Sturgis, whom a swift summons called from our side in all the beauty of his early youth. Motley was more nearly the ideal of a young poet than any boy —

APPENDIX E.

Mass. Hist. Society. Dr. Holmes's remarks.

for he was only a boy as yet — who sat on the benches of the college chapel. In after years, one who knew Lord Byron most nearly noted his resemblance to that great poet, and spoke of it to one of my friends; but in our young days many pretty youths affected that resemblance, and were laughed at for their pains, so that if Motley recalled Byron's portrait, it was only because he could not help it. His finely shaped and expressive features; his large, luminous eyes; his dark, waving hair; the singularly spirited set of his head, which was most worthy of note for its shapely form and poise; his well-outlined figure, — all gave promise of his manly beauty, and commended him to those even who could not fully appreciate the richer endowments of which they were only the outward signature. How often such gifts and promises disappoint those who count upon their future we who have seen the November of so many Aprils know too well. But with every temptation to a life of pleasant self-indulgence, flattery and the love of luxury could not spoil him. None knew better what they meant. 'Give me the luxuries, and I will dispense with the necessaries, of life,' was a playful saying of his, which is one of the three wittiest things that have been said in Boston in our time, and which, I think, has not been fairly claimed for any other wit of any period.

Mass. Hist. Society. Dr. Holmes's remarks.

"Soon after graduation, Motley left this country for Germany, where he studied two years longer in the universities of Berlin and Göttingen. I myself was absent from the country when he returned, and only renewed an acquaintance, which then grew to intimacy with him, after my own return from a residence in Europe, at the end of the year 1835. He was at that time just entering upon the practice of law, the profession which he had studied, but in the labors of which he never became very seriously engaged.

"His first literary venture of any note was the story called 'Morton's Hope; or, The Memoirs of a Provincial.' This first effort failed to satisfy the critics, the public, or himself. His personality pervaded the characters and times which he portrayed, so that there was a discord between the actor and his costume. Brilliant passages could not save it; and it was plain enough that he must ripen into something better before the world would give him the reception which surely awaited him if he should find his true destination.

"The early failures of a great writer are like the first sketches of a great artist, and well reward patient study. More than this, the first efforts of poets and story-tellers are very commonly palimpsests: beneath the rhymes or the fiction one can almost always spell out the characters which be-

APPENDIX E.

Mass. Hist. Society. Dr. Holmes's remarks.

tray the writer's self. Take these passages from the story just referred to: —

"'Ah! flattery is a sweet and intoxicating potion, whether we drink it from an earthen ewer or a golden chalice. . . . . Flattery from man to woman is expected: it is a part of the courtesy of society; but when the divinity descends from the altar to burn incense to the priest, what wonder if the idolater should feel himself transformed into a god!'

"He had run the risk of being spoiled, but he had a safeguard in his aspirations.

"'My ambitious anticipations,' says Morton, in the story, 'were as boundless as they were various and conflicting. There was not a path which leads to glory in which I was not destined to gather laurels. As a warrior, I would conquer and overrun the world; as a statesman, I would reorganize and govern it; as a historian, I would consign it all to immortality; and, in my leisure moments, I would be a great poet and a man of the world.'

"Who can doubt that in this passage of his story he is picturing his own visions, one of the fairest of which was destined to become reality?

"But there was another element in his character, which those who knew him best recognized as one

Mass. Hist. Society. Dr. Holmes's remarks.

with which he had to struggle hard, — that is, a modesty which sometimes tended to collapse into self-distrust. This, too, betrays itself in the sentences which follow those just quoted: —

"'In short,' says Morton, 'I was already enrolled in that large category of what are called young men of genius, ... men of whom unheard-of things are expected; till after long preparation comes a portentous failure, and then they are forgotten. . . . . Alas! for the golden imaginations of our youth. . . . . They are all disappointments. They are bright and beautiful, but they fade.'

"Mr. Motley's diplomatic experience began with his appointment as Secretary of Legation to the American Embassy to Russia, in 1840, — a position which he held for a few months only, and then returned to this country.

"In 1845 he wrote an article on Peter the Great for the North American Review, which suggested to many of his friends that, though he had not taken the place as a novelist he might have hoped for, there was in him the stronger fibre of an historian. He did not, however, give up the idea of succeeding in his earlier field of effort; and in 1849 he published his second story, — 'Merry-Mount, a Romance of the Massachusetts Colony'; which again, with all its merits of style and its brilliancy of description, was found wanting in some

APPENDIX E.

Mass. Hist. Society. Dr. Holmes's remarks.

of the qualities demanded by an historical novel, and settled the question for him that his genius was not in every way adapted to that kind of composition. The truth was, he could not divest himself of his personality and lose his individual character in that of his own creations. It will be noticed, that, while his first story turned on the adventures of an individual, his second story came much nearer to the complexion of a true history. It was at about this uncertain period of his career that a friend of his found him at work one day with a Dutch folio and a dictionary of that language. On being asked what he was doing with those uninviting books, he spoke of his turning his studies in the direction of history. 'I must break myself on something,' he said.

"What came of the studies which began with that Dutch dictionary you all know, the whole literary world knows, and I need not recite the story. Neither will I take up your time with criticisms upon those noble works, which have passed their ordeal, and stand among the foremost contributions of the New World to the literature of the Old. The personal enthusiasm which gives a glow to every page, the inborn love of freedom, the generous sympathy with all that is lofty, and the passionate scorn of all that is petty and base, the richness of his descriptions, the vigor of his por-

Mass. Hist. Society. Dr. Holmes's remarks.

traits, — to speak of these is to repeat the commonplaces of all our literary tribunals. I cannot refrain from adding a single thought which I do not remember having met with.

"The sturdy little State of Holland — a nation with a population comparable for numbers with that of the city of London — offers itself to too many English and American minds with the unheroic aspect in which the Dutchman has been presented in the satirical verse of Marvell and the ludicrous travesty of Irving. We cannot keep the pictures and figures of Diedrich Knickerbocker out of our fancies when we think of a Hollander. Mr. Graham, the English historian of the United States, complains that Mr. Irving 'has by anticipation ridiculed my topic and parodied my narrative.' We can still smile, or laugh, as Sir Walter Scott did, over the extravagances of our great American humorist; but it remained for an American historian to assert the true dignity of the valiant people who conquered an empire from the waves, and rescued it from the tyranny of still more lawless masters. The world can forgive all the playful mischief of the satirist so long as it contemplates the majestic figure of William the Silent, and reads the story of the defence of Leyden, the record of John of Barneveldt, and the romantic episode of Hugo Grotius in the pages of Motley.

APPENDIX E.

Mass. Hist. Society. Dr. Holmes's remarks.

"I shall not do more than allude to the further diplomatic career of our honored associate. I know that it ended in disappointment, and a feeling that a great wrong had been done him. But I know, also, that his highest office was undertaken with a profound sense of responsibility; that its duties were discharged as faithfully as he knew how to perform them; and that, whatever sting was left by the manner in which he had been dealt with, there was no poison of self-reproach to rankle in the wound. Those who will search curiously enough in the 'Life of John of Barneveld' will discover at least one passage in which the writer's own violated sensibilities find an expression in the record of another's grievance,—the natural device by which men and women of all ages have sought relief:—

'Πάτροκλον πρόφασιν, σφῶν δ' αὐτῶν κήδε' ἑκάστη.'

I do not believe that the violence which reached the nervous centres of Sumner's life told on him with more fatal effect than the rude shock of Mr. Motley's sudden recall from England upon his proud and excitable spirit, and through his sensibilities on the organ of thought, from the internal laceration of which he died.

"A slight attack—hardly serious enough in its effects to be called paralytic—interrupted the lit-

Mass. Hist. Society. Dr. Holmes's remarks.

erary labors which he had resumed after the close of his diplomatic career. His speech never seems to have been affected, and his handwriting showed no remarkable change, though he complained of weight and weakness of the right side, and found it a considerable effort to write. He was slowly regaining something of his usual health and spirits, when the death, in December, 1874, of the lovely and noble woman who had made the happiness of his life, cast the deep shadow over him which was never lifted. He passed the summer which followed his bereavement in this country, where for some weeks I saw him daily, and under those conditions which revealed his inmost nature more completely than I had ever known it in my long intimacy with him. He appeared to have forgotten all lesser trials in the one great sorrow which had left his life so nearly desolate. One thought, one feeling, seemed ever present; an undercurrent which betrayed itself not by unmanly signs of weakness, but by the tenderness and the reverence to which the memory of her from whom he had been parted saddened and subdued every accent. The language in which he spoke of his wife was the highest tribute to womanhood that ever found words on living lips in my hearing. And not to womanhood, not to that noble woman alone, for they revealed the passionate intensity of his own loving nature, and

APPENDIX E.

Mass. Hist. Society. Dr. Holmes's remarks.

showed us better than we ever understood before what was his peculiar underlying charm, and why we who loved him had loved him with such strong affection.

"But time has anodynes for griefs it cannot cure, and his letters showed that he was doing his best to bear his burden of sorrow, and that the affection of those who were left him was not without its healing influences. He had even hoped to be able to do something more in the way of literary labor, when suddenly, on the 29th of May, without any immediate warning, the thread by which his fate hung over him parted. The summons, though at an unexpected moment, might have been looked for at any time. The stroke fell like a blow on the already suffering organ through which his untiring intellect had wrought its vast and exhausting labors. 'It has come!' he said, and, after a few hours of unconscious life in death, he passed quietly away.

"He leaves all his uncounted honors, which I need not try to enumerate; he leaves the unblazoned record of a social career hardly rivalled for the brilliancy of its success; his works, sacred to heroism, the spirit of freedom and humanity, are his monument; and, amidst the sorrowing tears of those who dearly loved him, in many lands and in every station of life, from the lowliest to the lof-

Mass. Hist. Society.

tiest, he is laid by the side of her from whom he would not have been parted in death, to sleep in the mausoleum of a nation surrounded by the sepulchres of those who have made her history."

The Rev. R. C. Waterston then said: —

Rev. Mr. Waterston's remarks.

"It is a pleasant thought, Mr. President, to remember that the two members whom we to-day commemorate were personal friends. I have here a brief letter from Mr. Motley to Mr. Quincy, — the last letter which Mr. Quincy ever received from him, — written in pencil, from Nahant, during his last visit to this country. It may have some interest at this moment.

Mr. Motley's last note to Mr. Edmund Quincy.

"'MY DEAR QUINCY, — Many thanks for your kind words of remembrance, and for your Memoir of Charles Sprague. I perfectly remember our visit to the venerable poet, and am highly gratified that he should have been pleased by it. I have read your Memoir with much interest and sympathy, and should think it a very just, and not in the least an over-appreciative, tribute to his delicate genius and genuine and honorable character.

"'There are a good many lines of his poetry which I can repeat now, and could do ever since I was a Sophomore. I hope to see you in Boston before I leave, which will be in October, as people

APPENDIX E.

Mass. Hist. Society. Mr. Waterston's remarks.

seem to decide that the winter here will be too severe for me.

"Pray excuse my illegible pencilling, but it is very hard work for me to write.

"'I am your sincere friend,

"'J. L. MOTLEY.'"

Mr. Waterston continued: "Mr. Motley, after the publication of his 'Merry-Mount,' expressed his regret to Mr. Quincy that it had met with so little success. Mr. Quincy replied: 'Motley, turn your attention to history. Your style is admirably adapted to that, and every power of your mind would there find ample scope, and the result, I am sure, would meet with success.' 'Do you think so?' he said. 'I feel certain of your perfect triumph in that field,' continued Mr. Quincy. It is pleasant to think that these life-long friends went so nearly together. United in their lives, in their death they were not divided."

Professor William Everett then spoke as follows: —

Professor W. Everett's remarks.

"There is one incident, sir, in Mr. Motley's career that has not been mentioned to-day, which is, perhaps, most vividly remembered by those of us who were in Europe at the outbreak of our civil war in 1861. At that time, the ignorance of Eng-

Mass. Hist. Society. Professor W. Everett's remarks.

lishmen, friendly or otherwise, about America, was infinite: they knew very little of us, and that little wrong. Americans were overwhelmed with questions, taunts, threats, misrepresentations, the outgrowth of ignorance, and ignoring worse than ignorance, from every class of Englishmen. Never was an authoritative exposition of our hopes and policy worse needed; and there was no one to do it. The outgoing diplomatic agents represented a bygone order of things; the representatives of Mr. Lincoln's administration had not come. At that time of anxiety, Mr. Motley, living in England as a private person, came forward with two letters in the Times, which set forth the cause of the United States once and for all. No unofficial, and few official, men could have spoken with such authority, and been so certain of obtaining a hearing from Englishmen. Thereafter, amid all the clouds of falsehood and ridicule which we had to encounter, there was one lighthouse fixed on a rock to which we could go for foothold, from which we could not be driven, and against which all assaults were impotent.

"There can be no question that the effect produced by these letters helped, if help had been needed, to point out Mr. Motley as a candidate for high diplomatic place who could not be overlooked. Their value was recognized alike by his fellow-

APPENDIX E

Mass. Hist. Society.

citizens in America and his admirers in England; but none valued them more than the little band of exiles, who were struggling against terrible odds, and who rejoiced with a great joy to see the stars and stripes, whose centennial anniversary those guns are now celebrating, planted by a hand so truly worthy to rally every American to its support."

Remarks were also made by the Rev. S. K. Lothrop, D. D., and the resolutions were unanimously adopted, all the members rising.

The President appointed Professor Lowell to write the Memoir of Mr. Quincy, and Dr. Holmes that of Mr. Motley, for the Society's "Proceedings."

On motion of Mr. George B. Emerson, it was

"*Voted,* That the commemorative proceedings of this meeting be printed."

Appendix F.

List of his Honorary Titles.

APPENDIX F.

Honorary titles, etc.

THE following list of the Societies of which Mr. Motley was a member is from a memorandum in his own handwriting, dated November, 1866.

Historical Society of Massachusetts.
" " " Minnesota.
" " " New York.
" " " Rhode Island.
" " " Maryland.
" " " Tennessee.
" " " New Jersey.
American Academy of Arts and Sciences.
American Philosophical Society, Philadelphia.
Doctor of Laws, New York University.
" " " Harvard "
" " Literature, New York University.
Royal Society of Antiquaries, England.
Doctor of Laws, Oxford University, England.
" " " Cambridge " "
Athenæum Club, London.
Royal Academy of Arts and Sciences of Amsterdam.
Historical Society of Utrecht, Holland.

APPENDIX F.

Honorary titles, etc.

Historical Society of Leyden, Holland.

Doctor of Philosophy, University of Groningen.

Corresponding Member of French Institute; Academy of Moral and Political Sciences.

Academy of Arts and Sciences of Petersburg.

Doctor of Laws, University of Leyden.

The last honorary title conferred upon him was that of Foreign Associate of the French Academy of Moral and Political Sciences. This is the highest title the Academy can confer.

Appendix G.

Poems by W. W. Story and William Cullen Bryant.

APPENDIX G.

I CANNOT close this Memoir more appropriately than by appending the two following poetical tributes: —

IN MEMORIAM, — JOHN LOTHROP MOTLEY.

BY W. W. STORY.

Poem by W. W. Story.

Farewell, dear friend! For us the grief and pain,
Who shall not see thy living face again;
For us the sad yet noble memories
Of lofty thoughts, of upward-looking eyes,
Of warm affections, of a spirit bright
With glancing fancies and a radiant light,
That, flashing, threw around all common things
Heroic halos and imaginings;
Nothing of this can fade while life shall last,
But brighten, with death's shadow o'er it cast.

For us the pain; for thee the larger life,
The higher being, freed from earthly strife;
Death hath but opened unto thee the door
Thy spirit knocked so strongly at before;

APPENDIX G.

Poem by W. W. Story.

And as a falcon from its cage set free,
Where it has pined and fluttered helplessly,
Longing to soar, and gazing at the sky
Where its strong wings their utmost flight may try,
So has thy soul, from out life's broken bars,
Sprung in a moment up beyond the stars,
Where all thy powers unfettered, unconfined,
Their native way in loftier regions find.

Ah, better thus, in one swift moment freed,
Than wounded, stricken, here to drag and bleed!
This was the fate we feared, but happy Death
Has swept thee from us, as a sudden breath
Wrings the ripe fruit from off the shaken bough, —
And ours the sorrow, thine the glory now!

How memory goes back, and lingering dwells
On the lost past, and its fond story tells!
When glad ambition fired thy radiant face,
And youth was thine, and hope, and manly grace,
And Life stood panting to begin its race;
Thine eyes their summer lightning flashing out,
Thy brow with dark locks clustering thick about,
Thy sudden laugh from lips so sensitive,
Thy proud, quick gestures, all thy face alive, —
These, like a vision of the morning, rise
And brightly pass before my dreaming eyes.

And then again I see thee, when the breath
Of the great world's applause first stirred the wreath

Poem by W. W. Story.

That Fame upon thy head ungrudging placed;
Modest and earnest, all thy spirit braced
To noble ends, and with a half excess
As of one running in great eagerness,
And leaning forward out beyond the poise
Of coward prudence, holding but as toys
The world's great favors, when it sought to stay
Thy impulsive spirit on its ardent way.

For thee no swerving to a private end;
Stern in thy faith, that naught could break or bend,
Loving thy country, pledged to Freedom's cause,
Disdaining wrong, abhorrent of the laws
Expedience prompted with the tyrant's plea,
Wielding thy sword for Justice fearlessly, —
So brave, so true, that nothing could deter,
Nor friend, nor foe, thy ready blow for her.

Ah, noble spirit, whither hast thou fled?
What doest thou amid the unnumbered dead?
Oh, say not mid the dead, for what hast thou
Among the dead to do? No! rather now,
If Faith and Hope are not a wild deceit,
The truly living thou hast gone to meet,
The noble spirits purged by death, whose eye
O'erpeers the brief bounds of mortality;
And they behold thee rising there afar,
Serenely clear above Time's cloudy bar,
And greet thee as we greet a rising star.

Appendix G.

IN MEMORY OF JOHN LOTHROP MOTLEY.

BY WILLIAM CULLEN BRYANT.

Poem by W. C. Bryant.

Sleep, Motley, with the great of ancient days,
  Who wrote for all the years that yet shall be.
Sleep with Herodotus, whose name and praise
  Have reached the isles of earth's remotest sea.
Sleep, while, defiant of the slow delays
  Of Time, thy glorious writings speak for thee
And in the answering heart of millions raise
  The generous zeal for Right and Liberty.
And should the days o'ertake us, when, at last,
  The silence that — ere yet a human pen
Had traced the slenderest record of the past —
  Hushed the primeval languages of men
Upon our English tongue its spell shall cast,
  Thy memory shall perish only then.